GUILTLESS

TY, GUILTY, GUILTY, GUILTY, GUILTY, GUILTY, GUILTY, GUILTY, GUILTY, GUILTY, GUILTY, G
GUILTY, GUILTY, GUILTY, GUILTY, GUILTY, GUILTLESS, GUILTY, GUILTY, GUILTY, GUILT
ILTY, GUILTY, GUILTY, GUILTY, GUILTY, GUILTY, GUILTLESS, GUILTY, GUILTY,
LTY, GUILTLESS, GUILTY, GUILTY, GUILTY, GUILTLESS, GUILTY, GUILTY
ILTY, GUILTLESS, GUILTY, GUILTY, GUILTY, GUILTLESS, GUIL
ILTY, GUILTY, GUILTLESS, GUILTY, GUILTLESS, GUILTY, GUI
GUILTY, GUILTLESS, GUILTLESS, GUILTY, GUILTLESS, G
TY, GUILTLESS, GUILTLESS, GUILTY, GUILTLESS, GU
GUILTY, GUILTLESS, GUILTLESS, GUILTLESS,
SS, GUILTLESS, GUILTLESS, GUILTLESS, G
TLESS, GUILTLESS, GUILTLESS, GUILT
GUILTLESS, GUILTLESS, GUILTLESS,
GUILTLESS, GUILTLESS.
GUILTLESS!

GUILTLESS

John Nagy

ISBN-10: 0-9728504-1-4
ISBN-13: 978-0-9728504-1-4

For information or additional copies, write to:
John Nagy
4 Irvana Road
Rockport, MA 01966

This book is dedicated to my lovely wife Mary, with whom I continue to learn.

Contents

Preface

My journey to guiltlessness was a long one. It involved decades of painful mistakes, too much booze, fearful decisions, a lousy self-image, and not much self-respect. Today, however, I'm a lucky man. I have a fantastic wife, kids, an ex-wife who still speaks to me, and an extended family who are all still part of my life. My path to innocence was filled with obstacles and doubt, *but I got there*. Please believe that you can get there, too, and a lot faster than I did.

The purpose of this book is to share with you the truth about who you really are and to show you how to be in touch with that. It's time to free your *Self* from the guilty junk that seems to lurk deep inside. You may not even know that you doubt your own perfection and purity . . . but you do. Nonetheless, as you read the pages that follow, you will become convinced that what you always wished was the real "you" *is*, and that other one—the guilty one—well . . . *she/he never was*.

Take it from one who has been on both sides of the line—it's better on this side.

Won't you please come over?

Acknowledgments

As usual I couldn't have published a word without my dear friend and talented editor, Susan Shapiro. Susan has been there since "day one," and I am ever grateful for her participation and friendship.

I would like to thank my teacher, Tom Carpenter, and his wife, Linda. Both have contributed more than they will ever know to my life of peace.

Thanks to the best friends one could ask for, Don Doyle and Nancy Parsons, for their inspirational assistance on cover development.

My children Liza and Jake, Robin and Joey, grandchildren and extended family are always there for me . . . thank you all for bringing me to the awareness of love's presence.

I give special attention for beautiful book designing by Sherry Roberts, of The Roberts Group.

Blessings to my most beloved Melrose Group . . . don't forget to laugh!

All "guilt" feels the same.
I cannot feel yours and you cannot
feel mine, but we both understand
perfectly how each other feels
when we feel guilty.

Let this be the last
of the nightmare.
Let this, here at the beginning,
be the end of all
that is not peaceful.

"Guiltless" Is the Answer!

It always was, but we didn't know that. Since biblical times, guilt was assumed to be our natural state. Whether or not we subscribe to original sin doesn't really matter . . . somehow guilt ultimately finds its resting place deep within our consciousness, where it becomes a foundational cornerstone. For years now, people have come and gone from my office just outside of Boston, where we go into battle—me, insisting on their innocence, and they, defending their guilt. This is the way our sessions begin. If I'm lucky, I can convince a learner to trust my vision of them as being perfect, lacking nothing, and not being a victim of people or circumstances. Usually there is much resistance to my appeal for their innocence. Some, in time, will dare to trust the peace that innocence offers.

What Is Guilt Anyway?

Simply put, it is a way of life for most of us. It's an "umbrella" word that means defective, lacking something, damaged, corrupted, toxic, undeserving, sinful, unworthy, but ultimately, and most painfully, it means unlovable. Here lies the true power of guilt . . . the punishing nature of self-rejection. And when we reject ourselves, we're teaching the world that rejection is appropriate for us. Then others take our cues and learn to reject us as well. It is a fact that we are always teaching the world who we think we are. We draw people and events to ourselves according to what we think we deserve and, if that's according to a guilty self-image, then we're in for a rough ride.

Conviction is powerful—any conviction. When we believe something is true, our body language takes over. And if that conviction is guilt, the message becomes clear to others that we are not ready for unconditional love, for ease of living and happiness. Relationships, then, are often stressful and dysfunctional, and are a haven for frustration and miscommunication. The true purpose of any relationship is to learn just *who* we are. Instead of giving, we take from our partners, friends, and family what we desperately "need," which leaves others feeling used or unfulfilled. The self-image of littleness (guilt) cannot give or receive love, since love is not its priority; *survival* has become the priority and survival is fear-based. Love then, is never allowed to enter where fear rules. To put it simply, guilt prevents growth, denies love, assumes the need to manipulate, and self-rejects—a gloomy way to live. I know; I did it for decades!

All Too Often, We Don't Recognize That We *Are* Feeling Guilt

Unless we pay attention, other impulses can take over. A good rule of thumb is this:

Feelings that are designed to protect us usually have first condemned us, which leads to our needing protection in the first place.

Any feelings of fear, doubt, and, of course, need are really just confirming the assumption of guilt, which presumes that loss of some kind is imminent. Why wouldn't it be? The guilty deserve to lose. On some level, in our meek attempts at honor, we agree that we don't deserve to "win," to be abundant in relationships *or* at the bank. It would be so much easier if we weren't so willing to accept guilt, since then, the illusion of guilt would reveal its emptiness immediately. But, as we continue to protect ourselves against anything and everything, fear is documented by the mind, and guilt is allowed to steal our focus from a peaceful experience to a stressful one.

Why Do We Assume Guilt?

Many would say that to do so is humility, and therefore is righteous. Others maintain that Jesus died for our "sins," and that's enough to certify guilt. But most don't know why. I have learned that the presumption of guilt rests upon our experiences of condemning and judgmental thoughts, the effects of which "prove" that we are unkind and unloving. Since we are always aware of our mental processes, it's hard to imagine that one could feel innocent and loving in the presence of ongoing belittling thoughts of envy, rejection, disrespect, attack, defense, and so on. Literally, our thoughts are evidence of unholy behaviors and certainly seem to indicate a separation from the perfection of God (God as understood by you). After all, how many people actually see themselves as perfect, sinless and deserving? Very few, and so goes the continuous willingness to accept a diminished self-image — one *not* intended by Creation, or intelligent design, if you prefer. Even "random design" would have no purpose in feeling guilt since, *being random*, it has no purpose at all. How painful to live this way. Each thought compounds upon another, unfolding to the re-identification of unworthiness.

In a nutshell . . .

Our unattractive thoughts seem to prove our guilt, which is constantly reinstated by our acceptance of it.

4

Where Do Our Manipulating Thoughts Come From?

They come from our presumption of guilt; we need them for protection.

Acceptance of guilt expects punishment. Our manipulating defensive thoughts try to keep us safe, but confirm our guilty feelings at the same time.

You can see how circular this is. Guilty does as guilty is. The mind-set, which already sees itself as unworthy, will express this unworthiness in countless behaviors, none of which are attractive or loving.

Love needs nothing—guilt needs everything.
Love only gives—guilt only takes.

This is why unloving behaviors are always trying to get something, settle something, resolve something, escape something, or deny something. If you really stop and think about it, how often do you say something to a person that doesn't have some ulterior motive? Do you compliment someone because *you* need a compliment—because you are trying to seem "nice," or to soften another in order to benefit you in some way? Or do you speak from the heart, with absolutely no agenda or manipulation?

Generally speaking, most of what we relate to in others reflects something within ourselves that wants approval, acceptance and love. This "need" is just another way of verifying that love probably won't find its way to us unless we do something to arrange it. It's another expression of fear saying that we expect to get what we think we *really* deserve, which is anything but love and respect.

Where Do Angry Thoughts Come From?

Anger is no mystery. It is always fear in disguise. Anger (fear intensified) is a way of turning up the volume in order to make a point. Whether it speaks of victimhood, judgment, dissatisfaction, betrayal, etc. doesn't matter. Anger will take away the focus on oneself, and place the blame/need on another with the hopes of changing something in the relationship and, ultimately, to reduce fear. Many times, I have been "angry" at someone because he or she didn't understand what I was trying to say, either about my point of view or my feelings. In truth, if I'm misunderstood, I feel unseen and, therefore, devalued. This is fearful to me and cries out for some adjustment in *you,* in order for me to feel better. And as I am understood or accepted by you, my anger dissolves. But actually, it's my fear that relaxes, offering a lily pad of calm until the next upset comes along.

Anger is fascinating, in a way. The other night, I lay awake, watching my mind wander. I felt my anger. In thinking about my childhood, other cultures and countries, terrorists, thoughtless neighbors, the incompetent, unruly, and cruel—before I knew it, I was marveling that I didn't have much use for anybody. I was struck with my own free-floating judgment . . . me, a teacher of truth! I finally just *allowed* for the absurdity of my raging ego and went to sleep.

The next morning, I remembered those mindless meanderings and felt better for some reason. I felt softer and relieved that those crazy feelings were not really true, but the reflection of my fearful ego that was allowed to show itself in my "half-sleep" state.

In my view, it's important to be aware of how strong these angry feelings actually are, and how they stay hidden for the most part. But in order to let them surface, **we must agree not to punish them for being there.** In a technique called "focusing," we invite all feelings up to consciousness. We gently experience our feelings, thoughts, or beliefs regardless of how attractive or unattractive they may be. In this way, we allow the most *un*attractive parts of our subconscious to be seen and accepted.

It's a magical process during which everything that's inside is welcomed to the outside. Only then, will our deepest fears and guilts reveal their private secrets—without the risk of being punished. In focusing, we voluntarily take an internal inventory, adopting that wonderful principle that says, "When we look, we see." And what we see is freedom from our self-image of defect.

An easy exercise suggests that you:

▶ Sit quietly and imagine that you have entered that intimate feeling-center within.

▶ Now, gently invite any feeling that wishes to be expressed.

▶ Ask it to identify a name or phrase that best describes the feeling.

▶ Then, be willing to feel the full extent of it without resistance or judgment.

▶ In a few moments, it will fade, and you can invite another feeling into focus.

The purpose is to allow all feelings to be experienced without you feeling "beaten up" by yourself for having them. After all, they're just feelings, not facts.

See Them – Free Them!

Sometimes, miracles happen. We may not know why, but if we are available for healing, they just do. Our innermost guilts and fears are literally ashamed of themselves for being there. Our minds are also ashamed of harboring those thoughts. It's sad, in a way, that we seem to be victims of our own thinking. But the remedy is so easy: Let the feelings and thoughts speak, and we are suddenly in touch with our own innards. The relief this brings is like magic. An old Sufi poem says,

> Let it near
> Let it in
> Let it be
> Let it go

This really says it all. When we agree to look, we will see the truth right before our eyes. We will see those parts of our psyche that need healing (forgiving), and we will feel more integrated. It's impossible to feel "whole" when we are hiding from our own insides — when we are hiding from the part of our minds that believe crazy thoughts of guilt and judgment. That's why we are encouraged to nestle up to our *whole selves*: the good, the bad, and the ugly. Looking begets seeing and seeing brings clarity. Clarity gives us a choice to accept our own loving nature and deny the reality of defect. Remember, if it doesn't feel peaceful, comforting, or forgiving, it's false and doesn't really exist at all.

There is an amazingly simple tool you can use to determine whether or not your thoughts are speaking accurately about you. It's so simple, but so reliable. Here is the natural law:

Feelings immediately follow thoughts.

▶ If the feeling you have is unpleasant, toxic, guilty, leaves you feeling weak or regretful, or is demeaning in any way, **the thought that preceded it is false.**

▶ If the feeling you have is peaceful, loving, embracing, and supportive, **the thought is true.**

This is the most amazing barometer at your fingertips. It can be used for any circumstance, person, memory, dilemma, or decision. I have never experienced an occasion when this powerful axiom didn't work perfectly.

Try it now: Think of something—some memory or thought from the past when you wish you had acted differently. How does that feel? See how you have a "bad" feeling immediately? Now, the "bad" feeling is telling you that you did something or said something wrong. This, a priori, makes *you* "wrong," or "guilty." This guilty feeling is powerful when you believe it and will convince you on the spot that you have a long way to go before you can claim innocence.

Now, try it the other way. Think of something from the past that was wonderful . . . a person who loves you . . . a great time with friends or family. How does that feel? See how immediate your feeling-response becomes the central focus? It picks up where the thought leaves off. This lovely feeling is telling you that you were "OK" in the thought-memory — that you were "good." And doesn't it feel good to be good?

To use this as a basis for self-discovery, you must identify the specific feeling that is speaking. If, for instance, you regret having spoken in anger and hurt someone's feelings, it would be easy to accept that you are an angry person, which only makes you guilty again. But looking closer, you can ask, "*Why* was I angry?" You will see the answer immediately. You were frightened about something. You either felt misunderstood yourself or compromised in some way. This could lead to disapproval or rejection of you by the other. That was the actual fear . . . *that you would lose love.*

"All you need is love . . . etc."

That is always the problem. By nature, we only want to love and feel loved. There is no other purpose. We crave either self-love or unconditional love from another. Love is the driving force behind everything. Behind peace and war, marriage and divorce, having children or making money, there is the search for love. All decisions are made to bring that "feeling" of accomplishment (self-love), success (self-love), safety (self-love), relationship (self-love through love for another), intimacy (self-love through love from another), etc. *All* positive feelings are only self-love; guilt, then, results in the withholding of that love — your own love from you.

Love Withheld

This is the most painful form of self- punishment. I remember a very sad event that took place in my first marriage. There is no question that I made mistake after mistake back then, but this particular memory I will never forget. My wife at the time was extremely capable and somewhat dominant in personality (at least I felt she was). Anyway, it always seemed like she had the upper hand, and I was always on the losing side of any discussion or argument, usually an argument. In this case, I don't remember what the issue was, but I do remember losing again. Subsequently, the only effective weapon left for me was what I always resorted to . . . punishing her. This time I was really angry, so I set out to give her both barrels.

Here was the plan: I would not initiate any discussion unless there was some urgent issue regarding the children, utility shut-off, health emergency, and the like. I would say "hello" when entering and "good-bye" when leaving, but nothing more. Not a word did I utter regarding the weather, what's on TV, who called, or even, "How are you?" Nothing! I said nothing. Not only that, I refused to get close enough to her to have any possible bodily contact. Going through a doorway at the same time, I would shrink back into a shadow. And sleeping at night . . . I couldn't have been closer to the edge of the bed without hitting the floor. I remember driving to Connecticut for the weekend with the kids, for three hours, and saying *nothing.*

This went on for almost three weeks. Then, she finally noticed. I had won . . . she cracked, and screamed, "What the f's the matter with you anyway!?" Well, you can imagine how that discussion unfolded. I argued my point from three weeks before, and she made her usual salient points. We got nowhere as usual, but I felt a renewed sense of power in my victory in the punishment game.

But now comes the truth: I suffered. I was miserable the whole time . . . miserable at my job and at home, miserable with the kids and with myself. I suffered the most intense loneliness of my life even though I was in a beautiful house with a wife and two great kids. The fact is, I experienced a kind of spiritual death.

Eventually, when I sobered up in Alcoholics Anonymous in 1986 and put together a few honorable months of inner work and therapy, I understood what actually took place during my three-week domestic skirmish. *I had experienced the devastating effects of my own withholding.*

It was *my* love that had disappeared from me.
I was the one emotionally starving for love.
I was the crucifier and the crucified.

I, as usual, was the loser!

Funny thing is that, at the time, I didn't understand why I was hurting so much. I hadn't yet learned that all love is self-love, that the effects of my behavior stayed with me, and that all content lies in the intent. But I was hurting enough to know that whatever was happening, my tactics were backfiring on me, and that had a lot to do with my ongoing frustration. It finally became completely clear that my manipulating intentions were bringing about hurtful outcomes that always seemed to land in my lap. Withholding in any form simply doesn't work.

Guilt must withhold.

Guilt Is the Punishment for Guilt

All the while I was withholding, I was suffering the guilt of doing so. In this way, my debt to "God" and the universe seemed like it was being paid. As a reminder, guilt feels like hurt, sorrow, grievance, anger, burden, shame, littleness, embarrassment, etc. We all have these unfriendly feelings much of the time, but now it's time to understand exactly what's actually going on when we do feel them . . . *punishment, nothing more.* It seems crazy that the penalty for being guilty would be more guilt, but that's what makes this circular nightmare so painful.

We think or do things that make us feel guilty. Therefore, we do not deserve to feel happy.

So we withhold self-love and self-approval, and experience the loneliness of guilt all over again. Around and around and around and around it goes—**the guilty circle of fear.**

There is no escaping the internal guilt-mechanism. If we are willing to believe in guilt on any level, then it will do its work automatically. Remember, to the ego, guilt is righteous. It pays the debt for unloving behavior. Ego keeps score, and whoever owes a debt for dishonorable actions or thoughts must pay, so that order is maintained, both internally and out in the world. Guilt, then, is the ego's stabilizer. Guilt makes us "even," since we are all too familiar with its power and application, and are all too ready to use it.

"Passive" Withholding

Understanding the effects of what I call "passive withholding" requires a real willingness to grow. Passive withholding isn't overt. There is no conscious intent to wound the other; no penalty is being delivered. But unfortunately, there is no consistent loving message being delivered either. I had someone in my office today who, with some painstaking dialogue, finally admitted that he was passively withholding from his wife. Every day by *not* going the extra mile to convey respect, caring, and value to her, love was being withheld. Yes, he was always courteous, supportive when "necessary," and committed for the long haul, but still she suffered as though alone. And all the while, he just couldn't understand what her problem was.

The struggles between them continued to grow fiercely as her underlying anger grew. It felt to her that he was above her, more intelligent, more capable, less crazy and moody, and generally superior. This condition, which persisted for over a decade, sabotaged any possibilities of affection or improved communication between them. So what was he doing wrong?

Again, he was *not* grabbing every opportunity to build her up and, at the same time, turn down his own light. This is paramount: We, as social animals, have a responsibility to be aware of the effects of our own behavior toward others. If I'm so focused on shoring up my own image to those around me, they become smaller. Wisdom (love), on the other hand, would seek every opportunity to become sensitive to the feelings of the other person and support a more equal self-mage for *them*. But this unconditional giving can only occur when we are centered in our own wellness, our own innocence and worthiness—**in our guiltlessness.** But if we are inwardly conflicted with guilt and fear, *we have nothing to give to another but our own thirst for support.* Plain and simple . . . the guiltless can give love freely; the "guilty" can only take it. I am happy to report that, in this case, this fine man has a true desire for healing and has changed his ways.

The Content Lies in the Intent
(An Essential Principle to Be Understood)

We have all seen people do things that are upsetting, and we often join them with our own ridiculous behaviors. When we get angry, lash out, and make judgments about others, we wind up feeling secretly ashamed (unless, of course, we run away from these feelings by denying our own "guilt"). The problem occurs when we take thoughts and actions at face value, and then judge them. It's a problem because we're not really judging the behaviors, but the folks who are acting them out. This accounts for all separation between people, regardless of circumstances—including intimate partnerships, international upheavals, business breakdowns, and internal unrest. All condemnation, anger, and judgmental positions result from our response to people or events, which always miss the point entirely. And the point is this:

When people act out through attack, defense, anger, withdrawal or judgment, they are only expressing fear.

When we understand that, they become innocent no matter the circumstances. We become innocent, too, and can finally put the attention on the real problem, which is never the actual behavior, *but the fear behind it*.

To see this more clearly, start by searching for the motive behind any action or expression. If you sense anger, judgment, criticism, rejection, or all-out attack, your willingness to see that it was fear that expressed itself—not guilt—will serve you in finding a peaceful solution.

A scolding mother is fearful that her daughter will be at risk unless her behavior changes.

A jealous or critical friend feels inadequate in your presence.

A judgmental neighbor feels that your presence will threaten him somehow since you may believe in a different philosophy of life.

Anger always means someone is afraid of losing something—love, money, stature, health, or life itself—and anger serves to send the message to "back off," thus protecting the threatened.

Just by seeing this, amazing things can happen. You will perhaps still be "put off," but you will not personalize the anger, judgments, etc., *and* you will have a chance to stop the problem from escalating through patience, explanation, or just plain kindness. At one time or another, we've all offered assistance to someone who is scared about something and, of course, it's easier when the anger isn't directed at us. Nonetheless, whoever is willing to take on the assignment of seeing *fear instead of attack* will find himself offering solutions rather than the old defense mechanisms, thereby bringing peace to all those involved.

How about today, just for fun, you depersonalize all unfriendly encounters and address the real cause. You won't be disappointed.

A Closer Look at "Intention"

"I love me." But what does this mean? It means that I recognize the meaning of my soul, my goodness, and my purpose, which is to be happy and fulfilled. This is where all power begins and ends. Absolutely anyone can be free, empowered, connected, innocent, and able to navigate through the world effectively if he is willing to take the reins and agree to complete responsibility for life, health and innocence. That is, in our willingness to direct our minds to serve our intentions, we will experience its limitless power to create without fear or doubt.

All decisions are creative, even those to suffer. Even to suffer stuckness or depression, anxiety or guilt, is to feel the power of Self, inasmuch as these choices will inevitably lead to healing, when enough suffering has occurred and we finally make the right choice for a different experience. All motion, therefore, is forward motion, and there is no such thing as "backsliding" or lost opportunities. When I say that our intention is to direct the mind, I mean that we are not victims of our own thinking contrivances or limited to our mind-set. *We can change anytime we want to.*

Your mind is a tool, designed to carve out of unlimited potential whatever your intent dictates. *Intent or motive is your will . . .* your inner voice making a decision as to where it will dedicate its energy. The mind simply serves the will and brings about in experience the directives you have chosen. This can seem unfriendly news since, if accepted, we are no longer allowed to be victims of our "limitations," damaged psyches, neuroses or dramas. Instead, we are asked to admit that our choices to experience these pains and limitations (deprivation of any kind) *are our choices.* The good news is that if we are *not* at the mercy of our perceived inadequacies, our past, our "limitations," then we can choose to experience new avenues of pursuit and finally become free to live life in a new way.

If you are wondering how to suddenly become a new person — a free spirit ready to create fulfillment — then examine this idea: Who limits you? Who holds you to a sub-creative standard? Who chooses to drink or use drugs, to attempt suicide, to hide in the background protected from those who might "hurt" you? Who chooses to procrastinate daily, to remain stuck in sameness, moving around and around in the maze? You/we do.

As we said, all experiences are chosen right now, in this moment, by the being that experiences them. All choices are voluntary and consensual. Resistance to believing this is expected, since it seems insane that one would choose a path of stuckness and fear. But if we are really honest about it, we can feel ourselves making these choices right now.

As you read these words upon this page,
doesn't it seem sensible that you have all the
control over your own life-path?

There is a request made to us in *A Course in Miracles* which says "choose again." This means *choose again.*

I recently counseled an older couple in marital work. She had attempted suicide several times and spoke of this as though she were helpless as to when or how such attempts might occur again. When I pointed out to her that these attempts at ending her life were silly, but worse, were aggressive acts against her husband, she turned white and sat silently, realizing for the first time that she *did* have a choice. All I needed to do was point that out to her, and soon she agreed to never use that vehicle again, since to do so was a violation against herself *and* her husband. To her amazement, she felt relieved that such experiences were finally over once and for all. As our work continued, both she and her husband learned that all anger, backbiting, and dysfunctional behavior in their relationship (expressions of guilt) could be surrendered simply by "wanting to."

This was the power of their "will" directing their minds to purposes of healing, and *not* depending upon the mind to provide constructive guidance. *The mind does not know how to advise you on matters of love and healing.* To expect *that* of our minds is a misapplication of the mind. Remember, the mind is a tool, and it will apply itself according to our instructions. In other words, it will do whatever we tell it to do. If it is the safety of old defensive ideas that we "will," then our minds will lend themselves to that conviction and we remain stuck. Again we are back to old ideas of survival, which include attack, defense, justifying, judging, demeaning, and other fruitless endeavors, all from the ego, and none able to effect growth and understanding.

Guilt has no power over your will;
it has no power over anything.

Go Inside and Ask

Sometimes it's difficult to convince one to trust this request, but I suggest that everyone try it. I have rarely come across a person who does not hear something, even if it's just a few words of encouragement. Just ask . . . in this moment . . . about a person or event, and see if you don't hear the gentle voice of your own Love/ Wisdom suggesting some solution or forgiveness to set healing in motion. This power I am asking you to tap into is an infinite well of information and guidance, all waiting for your willingness to use it.

When my kids were young, back in the eighties, we went to see the first *Star Wars* movie. What a thrill it was to dream about the "Force" and its power and goodness. I think everyone left the theater determined to connect to it the way we did. Well, truth is stranger than the movies, I guess, because you *do* have the "force"—your own private "force"—at your disposal. Think of it as the power of love, of all that is good, of truth and kindness, of wisdom and compassion. This *is* the force, *and it is waiting for you.*

What's fascinating about this power is its universal application. There is nothing it cannot do. If you have a problem in a relationship, ask, and the solution is at hand. If you desire to develop your career path, ask, and things start to happen. It's uncanny. Literally, the phone will ring, or you'll run into an old friend who will steer you to a new possibility. If you have a health problem, you will act appropriately and get the right kind of help.

There is nothing that cannot be corrected when a meaningful request is made.

It's useful to note here that the answers don't always come in a form that you will recognize. It may be that you will do nothing differently, but something will change, and the problem is either gone, or the relationship changes and the problem no longer needs solving.

There is a marvelous old song that Martin Mull wrote thirty years ago called,

"Jesus Walks Among Us Always." The chorus goes ...

*Jesus walks among us always,
sometimes big and sometimes small,*

*But if you can spot the small ways,
you can find him best of all,*

*It might be your little brother, Uncle Frank,
or Frankie's mother,*

*Or it may be on the telephone
that you hear Jesus call.*

The point is that we never necessarily know how the message or answers will arrive. Maybe an old friend, something you see on television, or a dream may trigger a new awareness, and, suddenly, you're off and running. So the crux of the matter is just to ask from the heart and be willing to hear the answer . . . and you will.

But Are We Willing to Believe That?

So much lies in the power of Mind (not the mind we think with, but *Mind* . . . that of consciousness). Many believe that Mind is all-powerful. When we capitalize the word *Mind*, we are recognizing the limitless creative potential *of* Mind. Of course it's essential that we accept that it is our consciousness that has all the power. We alone rule the universe, since all of its meaning comes from us. This is an essential metaphysical principle that we must embrace (more about that in a moment). The point is, when we take the responsibility of being in the driver's seat with respect to our own lives, no one else nor anything else *can* be held responsible. It's really all about us.

At first, you may find this an unfriendly idea—that we create the universe and all that it means to us—but if you allow it to sink in, this can bring relief to your belief in powerlessness. Think of it:

> *If we are able to create our own reality and*
> *all subsequent relationships, experiences,*
> *and outcomes, then we can change them!*

In other words, we can break it—true—but we can fix it, too!

I remember my first experience in Alcoholics Anonymous. I was aghast when I learned that my life was up to me, and that there was no one else to blame or to hold accountable for my circumstance. But, at the same time, it was so freeing to understand that whatever I had seemingly done to foul things up in my life, I could undo. This gives the ultimate freedom of choice, but we must be willing to choose for peace, forgiveness, and innocence. On the surface, that's a "no-brainer." But it's amazing how often we will settle for guilt when it becomes clear that, for us to be innocent, *everyone else must be too.* That presents a problem for the fearful ego mentality that literally survives by being stronger and less guilty than anyone else.

Let's face it—if everyone's innocent, then nobody's guilty. If that's true, we can't be victims anymore. And if that's true, then we never were! Now we can see the implications of taking full responsibility. We either condemn the world and ourselves along with it, or we free the world and ourselves.

There can be no compromise in this regard . . . innocent or flawed, all of us . . . one or the other.

Projection and Perception

(For the following, I must pay further tribute the wisdom once again found in *A Course In Miracles*. If you haven't ever heard of it, you have now. Find an *ACIM* meeting somewhere. Go to Google, type in "A Course In Miracles," and you will find a week's reading just in references and associated materials and resources.)

Projection/perception . . . what does that mean? Well, we all know what perception means—that which we "see" and understand according to our previous learning. Let's say, for example, that you see a youngster come up to a man, and say, sharply, "Come on, give me the money." The man backs up against the wall, shrugs, raises his arms submissively, and hands over the cash. The boy runs away. Immediately, you would assume some sort of pressure situation, a robbery perhaps—some sort of threat . . . *something* unpleasant for sure. Wrong. The boy was the man's son, and Dad had promised to buy him something. They met, and the boy, in a typically entitled way, demanded his due. Dad, in his playfulness, feigned helplessly to concede, and the rest is obvious.

But, at first glance, you could assume a robbery had taken place. You voluntarily projected the boy's intent, the man's victimhood, and "saw" a crime committed. Then, you "perceived" your own projection and became subjected to its message just as though it all came from the outside. But, in fact, the whole thing really came from the inside . . . of *you*, the projector.

It came from you, to you, voluntarily.

Now, pull back your focus from this example and look at your whole life. Literally *everything* you have ever surmised, thought, experienced, or believed came from you. Even as you read these words on this page, all the meaning they have *for* you is coming *from* you, according to what you desire to "see" right now. All experiences, then, are first chosen, and then are immediately attributed to some external stimulus or cause, making ourselves the recipient of the entire experience. This is the way we separate ourselves from taking full responsibility for everything that happens to us. We deny that we are the cause, and thereby are not held accountable. Sadly, then, daily routine experiences never have the chance to help us grow since we are always the victims *of* them. If anything, this routine only teaches more fear and doubt about the sanity of anything.

BUT . . . are we willing to see things differently? Are *you*, right here in the "now," ready to turn it around and say, "OK—this is *my* game, and these are *my* interpretations, and *I* can disengage from feeling controlled by my own projections, and choose to be guiltless instead"? Are you? Let's agree that you are. How do you do it? By *wanting* to.

Desire for Healing

Desire for a better way *is* what healing is. Desire determines your use for anything. *Your* desire can free you from your previously chosen world of conflict, guilt, and everything painful. By simply wanting a more comforting experience, you will have it.

Form follows function.

That is, form (which is any form of the physical or the abstract as felt) will serve either to punish or embrace, to soften or harden, to attack or forgive, according to your assigned application. It's amazing how simple this mindful powerhouse is.

Imagine how your life will be when you accept that *you* actually determine the meaning of all things around you, even the feelings inside of you. You will be able to see "ugly" behaviors as dysfunctional, not bad or sinful. You will relax and not have to be the punisher to those who suffer blindness to their own self-worth. You will forgive all thoughts, feelings, beliefs and projections that don't bring you joy since, now, you can direct understanding and patience to your own heart, instead of criticism and self-doubt. All this gives you the power to reinterpret the world out there and the one deep inside—both needing the wisdom and understanding from your Higher Loving Self (Mind).

This is the best way I know of to let the world off the hook for all pain and violence. If we are serious about taking responsibility for what we see and how we feel, we can first forgive ourselves for condemning and judging others, then everybody else for *their* fearful behaviors. Empowerment is rooted in the understanding that all meaning comes from the observer. Whatever I want to see, I will. From here, we can see guiltlessness instead of condemnation, and substitute assisting attitudes, which always promote learning.

Please, try this now with any thought or feeling you may have. Focus your intent to see it differently, to see your*self* differently . . . and you will.

A note here about desire: Often, your "will" can be misidentified as desire. "Will" or willfulness refers to the power of the mind to make things happen. Desire, on the other hand, directly reflects the heart or spirit from which all wisdom comes. Simply put, healing guidance is constantly offered from within; your willingness to respect and employ it is a function of your mind. It is this application of energy that makes things happen.

So it's a good idea to check in to your spiritual message center—your heart—and then bring on the elbow grease of your "will." What a beautiful combination when actualized. First comes the musical idea, then the expression of it through the stroke of the piano key. The idea originates as pure creative energy, then we apply the will to actualize the music: amazing!

Respecting your desire will never bring guilt.

Heaven or Hell – The Insanity of This

If there ever was hell, it could well be described as a guilty environment that happens *to* us . . . one that we do *not* make . . . where everyone ultimately pays for his or her sins. What's more, it truly is hell since, if we don't cause it, we are helpless to fix it. Imagine living with the idea that God (however you see that) creates you both "good" and "bad." This is insane. Since not only does the "bad" part of you act badly, but the good part of you feels guilty about it and, what's worse, is helpless to change it since it doesn't understand why it's both "good" and "bad" in the first place. Moreover, what kind of a god would create a conflictual being that would "sin," feel guilty for sinning, suffer penance as payment, then spend the rest of its life wondering if it paid enough to avoid hell after death? Want to be in hell? This is it.

So Why Do We Resist Letting Go?

Isn't it amazing how easily we relate to guilt, and how we resist the notion of only one world of innocence or love? It's a simple ego equation: We love what we made because we made it (*ACIM*). We think that by verifying our own silly beliefs of guilt, our minds that come up with these ideas are verified as well. By establishing reality in the *effect* (the notion of guilt), the *causes* (our minds and all they think) are seen as credible and, therefore, reliable. Seen the other way, the ego is convinced that if we doubt our feelings of guilt and unworthiness, then we somehow doubt our own minds, which leaves us lost without a compass in a world of impossible challenges.

If I can't depend upon my own mind, how will I live? How will I survive? How will I sleep at night? I guess letting go of guilt isn't so easy.

There's an example I often use to help us become willing to question our own thinking. You're trying to find your way to the ballpark. You stop and ask a stranger, "Which way to the park?" "Straight ahead, then right at the lights . . . you can't miss it," he says. An hour later, after driving around lost, you find yourself at your starting point, where the same fellow sits. It's obvious that he gave you the wrong directions. Do you roll down your window and ask him again? *No, of course not.* It would be ludicrous to ask that same man for instructions, as ludicrous as it is to rely upon the same mind that insists upon its own guilt for a solution *to* that guilt.

A guilty mind-set cannot see the singular truth of love. It holds two positions: love (which is dangerous since it abandons) and guilt (the absence of love). Neither represents reality since, in this experience, "love" is subject to fear and is weak. This is not love, but *conditional love*, which is unstable and undependable. It can abandon as quickly as it appears and, therefore, is punishing and dangerous. Conditional love always has a "deal" working in the background. The "conditions" must be met in order to allow "love" to be felt—conditions such as promises, guarantees, reciprocity, bargains, and everything else that requires quid pro quo. I will love you as long as you are safe, loyal, and exclusive. However, my "love" will turn to hate and punish you, if you f... me over in any way that compromises my safety. See how easy it is to understand how such conditions could never represent true love, and from this jaded point of view, who could ever find "love" safe?

What About These Two Realities?

How can truth (love) and falsity (the absence of truth or love) both be real? How can what's *true* and what's *not true* both be true? If there ever was an oxymoron, this is it. What *is* and what *isn't,* both vying for position. Preposterous. This mind is like the man who gave you the meaningless directions; it is unreliable and cannot solve the problem it creates.

Again, the fundamental reality is that love is the *only* reality. Reality, then, is truth, and where there is truth there can be no falsity. Where falsity is experienced then, there is only the nonrecognition of love's presence. *ACIM* refers to behaviors that reflect fear as "a call for love." The bottom line is that there *is* only love or a call for love . . . love extended, or the search for it—what a relief. The more we are willing to understand this, the more it's clear that whatever we have chosen . . . we *can* let go.

Letting Go

This is where the trouble starts; "letting go" means exactly what it says. It means no longer groping for solutions to guilt with the mind that causes it in the first place. It means opening to another resource, another "Voice," one from deep inside where guilty fearful ramblings are seen for what they are—nothing. This Voice is truly your own. This Voice is the Truth. This Voice is your Love, always speaking to you with an invitation for peace and clarity, and it is available to you whenever you are willing to hear it. I know it seems hard to believe that you have all the answers just waiting to be heard, but remember this: The answers you really need are not from your mind; they are from your heart. Your heart, in this case, can be associated with your *higher mind*, Truth, Love, Creation, the collective brotherhood, or any God you choose to identify with that brings you comfort.

It is essential that you now claim this guidance as legitimately your own, and not degrade its potential. **All** power lies in your agreement of deservitude, your birthright to Love's Presence. This power is limitless in its brilliance and wisdom. We've all heard stories of unfathomable courage and strength in times of need— the lifting of an automobile off a pinned pedestrian, the breaking of chains at the crucial moment, or the communication of urgency over great distances to one who cares. Well, this power has to come from somewhere, doesn't it? I can't explain it rationally, but if I say it's the power of Love that gets the job done, somehow we all can understand that.

*We can understand it because
we **are** the power of love!*

It is this same love that asks you to agree that you
are worthy of happiness and abundance. It doesn't matter what words you use when asking for help, or what
the circumstances are. In fact, the words *never* matter.
There is an eager loving assistance, which only wants
to help *you personally*, and needs only **your asking** to
activate your inheritance. But asking is essential. Asking is the signal that says, "I am ready to receive."
(Guilt can never be received since it does not exist.)

The Natural Laws of Receiving

Doesn't it seem a bit ridiculous to make a big deal about
"receiving"? One would think receiving comes easy.
After all, giving takes work, but getting is easy—right?
Wrong.

*Receiving requires a conscious agreement
that it is deserved.*

We all have an internal mind-set that secretly doubts
that we deserve anything good, whether it is love or
money. And don't kid yourself; the ego won't keep you
from getting what you need to survive, **but it will always get in the way of what you deserve,** which is full
abundance. This way, even the twisted ego's self-image
can live with itself by imposing limits on your fulfillment. Take this little test and explore your willingness
to receive.

Do I dare admit that I really want happiness?

This is always a risk. To consciously choose for peace and fulfillment is a setup for heartbreak in case it *doesn't* happen. Your ego knows this and will attempt to keep you from daring to reach out for life's riches. You surely won't get what you dream of by *not* asking, but at least you will be safe from more disappointment.

Do I deserve what I'm asking for?

You may answer, "Yes, I do," but deep inside, it's very possible that all the red flags are waving, "NO, YOU DON'T!"

Allowing...
As soon as you experience those red flags, no receiving can occur. You will always prevent what you want the most, since "honor" will not allow the undeserving to receive. This is because of your ongoing agreement to the ever-present reality of guilt. No changes are possible unless the fundamental change of innocence is allowed. This will set up further allowances as appropriate and will open the door to a whole new outlook where *no* limits on happiness exist.

We can't speak enough about these natural laws of allowing. Pay attention to how you really feel inside . . . are you really willing to let love in? Or do you need to keep a watchful suspicious eye out for any undeserved rewards coming your way?

The Softer Voice Is More Reliable

This is an odd concept, but generally true. The ego voice—that's the one speaking from fear—will yell and scream its defenses, objections, plans, or interpretations of everything that seems to be happening to you. It is a voice that is unmistakable to all of us as it barks out instructions from the helm. I know it's hard *not* to pay attention to these immediate impulses, but if we are willing to hold up for just a moment, another voice will speak and a more useful guidance will be heard.

The other voice will be softer in nature and its directive more reliable. This one will invite you to pause, forgive, embrace, include, accept, and trust. This one will tell you "what to do, where to go, what to say and to whom" (*ACIM—A Course In Miracles*). Imagine how wonderful it would be if all the answers to any question anyone could have were already present within, and all you had to do was to trust that? Well, that's a fact; you *do* have the answers within, and you need only to ask in order to hear. Too often, though, we interpret asking as "weakness." Men will often avoid asking for help or directions even when hopelessly lost, just to avoid appearing small. And if it's difficult for us to ask others for assistance or help, you can see how tough it is to ask something you can't see or touch—something amorphous and abstract like your "Inner Voice." We can easily understand how fearful the ego is of deferring to this and then losing control.

A gentle voice is guiltless.

Courage!

Try it—just go inside and ask. If you are comfortable with a "Higher Power," try that. If you use "God," the "universe," "Holy Spirit," or "Self," that's fine. It doesn't make a particle of difference what you call it. The clarity from within will come, and you will hear it because you are willing to. Wars throughout the centuries have been fought over whose "god" is *the* "god"—what *is* the power and *where is it located?* None of that matters. We all have the power of truth and love, the wisdom of the ages, at our fingertips when we turn away from our frightened egos and focus our energies toward a more reliable resource . . . the one inside.

Look at nature. Imagine what chaos would occur if the birds, bees, beasts, and fishes mistrusted their own inclinations! Dogs wouldn't bark, wolves wouldn't howl, the bugs would question their mating rituals and the fish would wander to the depths. Absurd. We all have a built-in compass for what is appropriate, for what has honor. It needs no approval nor does it need permission to take action. Trust what reveals itself from deep inside, and you will know the truth about yourself and everyone else. Love is real, and *you are that.*

Getting in touch with your inner guidance is essential for responsible living.

Fear: The Expectation of Loss

Fear is a little less obvious to see than anger because it's partially hidden by the anger. Fear is the expectation of loss. It has assumed that, one way or another, unlimited abundance is not coming because we don't deserve it. No one does. In our underlying belief that we shouldn't expect to be lovingly rewarded, the opposite view dominates. In fact, we will lose — we will lose everything, including love, money, respect, and, ultimately, life itself. This prevailing mind-set doesn't know exactly why loss is coming, but it believes it is nonetheless. It only makes sense, then, to delay loss of any kind as long as possible. Controlling others with countless codependent behaviors, our denial of responsibility, attacking, and withdrawal into isolation are but a few of the mechanisms designed to keep us "protected" from our fear.

But, why should we be fearful in the first place? Why should we expect loss?

Because we think we are defective, toxic,
damaged, corrupted, violated, unworthy,
and anything else you can think of that
diminishes our stature.

Again, the umbrella word for all of these beliefs is guilt. The belief in guilt overrides the rationale. Beliefs can't think. They don't know anything. They simply believe. One thing is for sure, though — *as long as you agree with these beliefs in guilt, their effects will remain!*

Here is a little formula that I often use to help understand how all this works:

▶ Anger is the leading edge of fear.

▶ Fear is the expectation of loss.

▶ Expectation of loss reflects the conviction guilt.

Or seen the other way . . .

> Belief in guilt leads to expectation of loss—
> which leads to the experience
> of fear—which results in all forms of
> anger!

There is an old saying bandied about regarding the nature of fear. I think it originally came from *ACIM*. It says, "Don't be afraid of your fear." Now, this is easy to say, but not so easy to do. The wisdom it carries, though, will spare you many calories of intense stress. The meat of the concept refers to the actual unreality of fear itself. Since guilt is completely fictitious, *all that stems from it is fictitious as well*. We should take comfort in at least knowing that the fear being felt is not real, but *is* trying to convince you that it is. To the ego, fear is important and must be "true" in order to stabilize the foundation for littleness and defect.

This is always important to the ego, since it first looks for evidence that will support judgments against others as a way of diverting responsibility for pain **to** some*one* or some*thing* else—from Creation on down to people, places and things—so that it can continue to condemn and justify its anger. But the truth is that, when "guilt" is dispelled through Vision, all blame disappears, and people, places, things, and events become innocent and, of course, so do you. (Read this until you see it!)

Unfortunately, all too often the readiness to assume guilt pervades. There is nowhere in the human experience where the feeling of guilt hasn't invaded. In fact, many brilliant teachers of metaphysics maintain that the entire experience of the physical world (one of bodies that live and die) is itself a statement of guilt. Conversely, spiritual "Oneness" or "Wholeness" presumes an eternity of happiness and love, unencumbered by the limitations of bodies that die and all other forms that are temporal.

When you accept this advanced reality, life in the world can become the laboratory where *belief* in guilt is recognized and, therefore, remedied. Here is the only sensible use *of* the physical world—to recognize the belief in guilt and put it to rest for all time. We enter this "lab" in order to get a handle on just how much we actually believe we are "sinful" and undeserving. When seen and understood, we can do something about it.

But if we continue to live in denial of our innocence and stay unwilling to see through our guilty delusions, they will remain intact and continue to divert our energies away from healing to mere survival in the world of conflict.

Fear of Loss Never Saved Anything

That's the truth of the matter. If we accept the premise that *all content lies in the intent*, and that *only love is real*, then there can be no real content in anything fearful. (I know you can make an argument for the usefulness of fear, and I will address that in a minute.) "Content" refers to reality. "Reality" is anything that is substantive, which will always refer to, or assist in, the expression of Truth. Gestures that are intended to reveal one's *True Self* in relationships of any kind—from intimate to casual—are representing real content and meaning. Conversely, empty gestures designed to bring about specific results in order to remain safe, protected, or insulated are lacking in truthfulness and honor and, therefore, have no content whatsoever. They are not "bad" per se, but they *are* meaningless.

We have all feared loss, though. In fact, my entire life was dedicated to minimizing loss since I fully expected to get my "ass kicked" one way or another, either financially, physically, or through some sort of humiliating nightmare. Let's face it—we're all afraid of loss on some level.

It sounds ridiculous to say that "loss is unreal" since we can all relate to having lost, or so it seems. But, did you really lose? Or, did you learn what doesn't work?! Yes, that's it. Past losses are clear-cut demonstrations of what *doesn't* work. I can guarantee you that if you hadn't "lost" that investment, that friend, that whatever, you wouldn't have learned a damned thing. Why would you ever learn anything unless there was some perceived consequence for the wrong choice? But the trick is to see consequence as teaching—*not punishment!*

All relationships, whether they are personal or business, that "fall apart" were never meant to be permanent in the first place. This is so simple it hurts. If you are willing to believe that your fear of losing anything is a waste of time (since you're meant to have, not lose) then you're always safe. This means that if you are meant to have something, you will. But if you're better off without it, it will go or will never come to you in the first place. It will always be as it was meant to be. Any and all worries, then, are unnecessary. This takes away any need for planning against loss or protecting yourself against anything **ever again.**

Remember—Love is always appropriate,
and knows what you need.

You Can *Always* Depend Upon Love

Oh, how I wish I could wave a magic wand and have you immediately accept this! Believe me when I swear to you, that the entire problem of inner conflict can be resolved with an unconditional acceptance of this simple truth.

Let's say it again:

You can always depend upon love.

If I say to you, "Don't worry; the truth will set you free" or "Take it easy, friend; it will all work out in the end," you might find some relief in that. Well, in that moment, you trusted the power of Truth and allowed for the possibility that it will all make sense some day. That's no different than trusting love's essence to pave the way to sanity without your direction. Love has its own agenda, and that is to free you and everyone else from another moment of suffering.

Many times in my office people say, "John, give me something to hold on to till next time."

I invariably say, "Hold on to your own wisdom; hold on to your own love, since it alone knows how to help you."

And they will say, "Yeah, yeah, I know, but give me something tangible." Tangible . . . are you kidding? What could possibly be more tangible than your own desire to love and to feel loved? Remember, when you feel OK with yourself, nothing can challenge that. No incoming b.s. from the outside world could possibly affect you. You become immune to doubt and will never again be subject to the old ways of using people to feel worthy. You won't need to, since worthiness from now on will gush from you like a fountain of nourishment — clear, sweet, and wonderful. Don't ever question again whether or not your love is dependable.

Dependable is what love is.

Pain

Looking at "loss" a little closer brings us to the heart of the matter . . . pain.

Pain is the predisposition to suffer by consent.

But what is suffering? A few pages ago, I talked about the withholding of love. It turns out that all painful and hurtful feelings *are* exactly that. The withholding of self-love is the *only* way by which we can feel punished. I had a difficult time accepting the idea that *I* am the punisher and the punished. Why would I do that to myself? Because I believe I deserve it.

Since pain is always chosen by the experiencer, then punishment is appropriate according to our own self-image; we know that now. But there is another reason to choose pain — it's comfortable and familiar. For example, let's go to prison for a minute. A prisoner gets out of hand and is sent to solitary confinement for a month. Suddenly one day, the door opens, the light shines in, and the guard says, "OK, chump, back to your cell."

Now, one would think this would be a huge relief for the inmate, but something strange often happens. Back in his cell, he backs into the corner. He closes his eyes and with his hands extended, desperately tries to feel the walls pushing in. When he touches the walls, he gently pushes out. He has recreated solitary confinement where the boundaries were clear and understood, and feels the safety of that.

This reaction to "freedom" shows that change itself is terrifying. It doesn't matter that it's a change for the better . . . any change can be problematic because you can't bring the old "m.o." with you. "At least, here in my tiny dark cell—in my heartache, guilt, and littleness—I know the deal. I won't be happy, but I'll be safe."

What a pity to stay hidden, away from the "light." Of course, the ego sees this as some sort of internal measure of honor. After all, we *are* willing to suffer, sometimes even silently. And in a perverse kind of way, we can earn "honor" this way. But don't kid yourself . . . this is an absolute dead end. Self-confinement in secrecy, shame and fear is not only solitary, it's a kind of execution, since every day in hiding is another day that will be just like yesterday. There is nothing honorable about this kind of pain. Pain will never lead one to honor.

The funny thing is, you are already honorable . . .
it doesn't have to be earned.

Honor

I find it fascinating that one's "honor" is everywhere, even in the feeling of guilt. It's because we *are* honorable that we choose guilt in the first place, since it represents our awareness that something in our behavior isn't quite right, and we admit to that . . . that something we said, or did, or thought wasn't completely truthful. But in spite of that awareness, the old mechanism of transferring blame to others comes into play, since we still believe that we can and will lose if discovered. So we hide in the shadows behind a shield of even more dishonesty and defensiveness to the extent of being unkind if necessary.

Projecting guilt to those around us works for a while as we buy into our "justified anger" and victimhood, but sooner or later we always seem to face the music and default to that old guilty feeling. Our honor demands that we withhold self-love and suffer the punishment due. Ironically, this is an obtuse reflection of our knowing the difference between what's right and what's false, and we *do* know the difference. It's a bizarre kind of comfort to the "guilty" since at least we have the guts to take our deserved medicine. The ego can buy a little time with this nuttiness, but eventually we must become willing to see the emptiness of this game.

There can be no guilt in honor, nor honor in guilt.

Now Comes a Different Kind of Honor

Honor is one of those abstract words that are tough to define. We use words like ethical, good, decent, accountable, reliable, and a host of others to define honor. Let's try this definition:

Honor is that which you know instinctively but often fail to honor!

Funny, but true. We always know how to tell the truth, admit our fearful errors, and agree to adhere to more honorable guidelines. We know this because we're born with it; it's part of love's agenda to honor and serve the truth. In the marital vows, we "honor" a commitment. As children, we learn to "honor" our parents. But sadly, as we grow up, we experience what if feels like to *dis*honor ourselves.

Honor is like a committee of wise men and women deep inside, quietly offering guidance and advice. Unfortunately, in order to stay safe, we usually override our own wisdom and muscle into decisions and behaviors for all the wrong reasons. Don't worry about this too much, though; your honor committee never runs out of gas. It's always rarin' to go with just what you need to hear in every moment of your life. But we must start listening to get the benefits being offered.

How many times have you heard someone say, "if only I had trusted my gut feeling," or "I wish I had listened to your advice," or "I knew it was wrong but I did it anyway"? Honor was knocking at the door, but you wouldn't let it in.

A conscious commitment to listening is all it takes to change your life forever.

Pay attention to that beautiful, internal, soft but reliable voice which first says, "I love you," then offers its guidance. Honor is yours for the taking. Honor is your name. Thank God for honor. And, by the way, we don't deserve pain (self-punishment) for our errors; *we deserve forgiveness.*

Forgiveness

This is my favorite. Forgiveness by the traditional understanding says that you have first offended me, and now you expect me to release you from guilt. But that flies in the face of everything I've said so far. If we see guilt as unreal, what's to forgive? *Nothing.*

I know what you're thinking now—you're saying:

"No consequences for misbehaviors?"
"We all get off scot-free?"

Yes, there *are* consequences, but not as currently understood. Punishment in exchange for errors teaches *only* that one is guilty for having acted improperly either through the committing of a crime or some unkind gesture. *Correction,* on the other hand, teaches that there is another way to live, act, and treat others. Correction understands that all misbehaviors are only expressions of fear and defense, and do not speak to the relative goodness and deservitude of the individual. In plain English, *all* behaviors that are seemingly ugly and attacking are simply calling for understanding and love, *not* punishment.

Remember, early on we said that "guilty does as guilty is"? Well, guilt, shame, and fear will always try to protect itself through manipulations, anger, and attack; that's the nature of guilt. Our job as new cadets in the field of learning is not to respond in kind, but to take a breath instead, and recognize a "call for love" when we see one.

Look back on your own life . . . do you see something that isn't too pretty? Did you say something that was hurtful or worse? Did you hide some behaviors because you were ashamed to have them be known? Did you take advantage of another because you needed what you took? Sure, most of us have done these things, and the rest of you are lying.

However, *whatever* we did that wasn't "kosher" was done out of fear—fear that we needed protection from being revealed as "not good," fear that our point of view wasn't being heard, or fear of lack which, at the time, was handled by taking from another. No matter how you slice it though, it's your fear that made you do it . . . **not** some dark evil component inside that reeks of defect or sin.

Yes, there *are* consequences, and we have to own up to what protocol asks. That could be anything from an apology to a jail sentence . . . but one thing is for sure . . . guilt is not among them!

"Love Is Always Appropriate"— The Answer to Fear

Now, let's address the issue of fear as a useful influence for practical living. You could say that stopping at a red light is a fear-based action, since to not stop would most certainly result in disaster. Yes, that's true. But now it's time to bring out a powerful axiom that never fails to protect and carry one throughout life:

*Love is always appropriate,
even in a world of chaos.*

There is nothing complicated about this. Love, or the power of love that comes from deep inside, always knows the right thing to say and do, how to react, where to go, and how to feel. So, when trusted, Love (Truth) will always stop at the red light since, to do so, is to respect the customs and protocols we have established in the world. We agree to abide by the common sense we have all learned to trust. When we turn on our loving "automatic pilot," we will make appropriate decisions without struggling through an internal discussion of which way will be "safer." We know what's best, since another influence (one from deep inside) is guiding us through life now, one that offers appropriateness in all situations and relationships.

There is nothing as beautiful as moving through life free from fearful alternatives, but to do so requires your willingness to be "led" rather than to lead . . . and this requires *trust*.

Trust

"Trust" is one of those words that carries the wisdom of the ages but is so abstract that it's like trying to grab a cloud. Trust, faith, and belief all mean the same thing, but carry nuances subject to interpretation by the user. When I trust, I feel willing to accept my gut feelings about what's wrong and what's right, and I don't depend upon needed outcomes in order to feel safe. Outcomes, then, are free to unfold normally. In this way, we are freed from needing to control any*one* or any*thing* according to our fear-based agendas. A great man once said, "There is nothing to fear but fear itself." No truer words were ever spoken. They mean that through trust, our intentions and best interests will always be served. When we allow life (Love) to flow without strong-arming and fearful control, *happiness presides*.

There is a great moment in the Harrison Ford movie *Raiders of the Lost Ark* when he must cross the abyss to the Holy Grail in order to save his father. There is no obvious way to make it across, and as he stands there—frozen with fear—he hears his father's trusted voice whisper "trust." And so he does, by taking a step off the cliff into nothing. Suddenly, the ground comes up to meet his foot. Then another step, and again the ground appears to meet his foot . . . over and over until he reaches the other side. There is no logical explanation for this extraordinary example of trust, but for some inexplicable reason, we all seem to know what happened there. It's like being in love; we're not sure how we know, but if we are, we do! Trust . . . and find your power within.

What Is Guilt, Again?

Recently I gave a talk titled "Guilt Makes Fear — Fear Makes Guilt." What could be more circular than that? But it's true. When you are "guilty" about anything, fear is on the way. Maybe it's useful to revisit what guilt stands for — sickness, pain, death, doubt, grievance, upset, attack, defense, abandonment, rage, insult, loneliness, isolation, rejection, unworthiness, loss, loneliness, feelings of delusion, etc. In fact, all experiences or feelings that are *not* of love are the effects of guilt. In a way, this makes our job a little easier; we need only to notice if we are happy or not! Guilt, then, is the recipe for unrest and pain. And as long as we are willing to put up with this abstract, distorted nightmare, it will continue to capture its victims.

I find it difficult to imagine that guilt comes from "God," or that "Lucifer" could evolve from the same source. Do all living things experience guilt? Do they *have* guilt whether or not it's experienced? Does a plant have guilt? Does a hamster, a honeybee? From that point of view, guilt seems ludicrous . . . and perhaps it is. But it sure doesn't seem ludicrous when you look in the mirror and see a guilty reflection. After all, the mirror can't lie . . . or can it? In truth, *it* will never reflect the guilt that cannot exist, but *you* will misuse the mirror and distort its message. *You* will make chaos out of order, impurity out of perfection, guilt out of nothing.

The good news is that guilt is revealed as nothing more than the feeling one undergoes immediately after confirming the "reality" of a guilty thought — *any guilty thought.* It's essential to get this: Your guilty thoughts determine that the mind that's thinking them *is guilty.* That's the trap

Think of something from the past that you feel guilty about. Do you have it . . . that *feeling? That's guilt!* It's the visceral experience of the thought. In *A Course In Miracles*, a line reads, "All thought expresses itself in form on some level." That can be an expression of anger, attack, or defense; a feeling of inner sadness or unrest; or it can be "stuffed" down out of view only to be felt later on. Any way you slice it, you have paid the price by feeling something uncomfortable.

But the real point here lies in how readily we consent to *accept any punishing thought* as real or significant. We must see that clearly. There can be no reality in a punishing thought, since punishment itself is only the momentary withholding of your own love. And there can be no reality in withholding since it doesn't pursue a healing interest or express clarity, truth, and love. I know this seems conveniently simplistic, but we must retrain our minds to see the emptiness of guilty experiences, and then refocus to innocent and loving alternatives. Until our willingness to unhook from the willfulness of the "guilty ego" becomes resolute, peace will always be disallowed.

> *When we deny the reality of a thought that isn't followed by a peaceful feeling, we're freed from the feeling of guilt that is perched and ready to move in.*

When Did This All Begin . . . This "Guilt Thing?"

Well the ego (remember, the ego is just another guilty thought) would have you believe that guilt was born long ago, in the past. As we said, the Bible refers to original sin, placing the burden of error back in the Garden of Eden. And even as we experience ourselves in the "here and now," we still tend to look back to some place or time when we failed to be righteous, when we failed to avoid behaviors that "proved" our guilt. And, of course, we look to our early childhood where abuse and victimhood were born, setting up the expectation of continued disappointment and stuckness.

But Is That Really Where Guilt Comes From . . . The Past?

This gets tricky. If we say that it does come from the past, then we're doomed for sure, because we cannot go back to the past to undo it. The past is in the past, and that's that.

But, when some guilty memory from the past is tolerated even for a moment, that old familiar feeling will follow, and we've accepted our guilt in the present simply by not challenging it.

It's like a storyline. The salient points of the story are cemented in the past, and this gives a foundational backdrop for whatever is happening through the story up to the present. It's a perfect setup for feeling bad right now about something from long ago — or yesterday, for that matter. From this point of view, everything that is happening *now* is a development from yesterday, last week, and eventually from decades long gone by. The problem this creates is unsolvable: If the present is formulated in the past, then we as beings are literally authored in the past. This dashes all hopes of being renewed in the now, since, wherever we go, we drag our storyline along behind.

Many books have been written about this "being in the now" question. Some teach how to become freed from the past; others simply deny the past, as though it never occurred, thereby freeing one from its effects. This is getting closer to what works for me.

Whatever happened in the "past" was only meaningful if, at the time, your experiences represented the truth (love).

The "Truth," when capitalized, always refers to Love. Love, then, and Truth are synonymous. Love is True, and Truth is Love. I know this seems to be using one abstract reference to define another, but there is no other way to refer to Love and do it justice (more about the nature of love later on). Anyway, back to the past. As you remember different times, places, and events, you will have a feeling immediately following whatever it is you saw in your mind's eye.

For example:

Think of something from yesterday, or last year.
Be "there" for a second. How does that feel?

Well if you're anything like me, it's a mixed bag. There is some joy perhaps, but sadness too. Maybe something ended that you loved, or an opportunity was missed. Perhaps someone helped you out . . . or you them. Regardless of the situation, the feelings you feel inside tell it all.

If you feel happy, it means that there *was* love or "truth" there. But if that suddenly changed to sadness, then your contention is that love "leaves." Now, you have experienced loss. This seems to prove that love is whimsical. It comes and goes. It joins, then abandons. This kind of love is dangerous and, therefore, must be controlled. Ego has also "proven" that guilt has real staying power.

The point is this: If your memory serves to confirm that love in the past was painful in any way, then your mind reasons that love itself is unstable. And, since we've already said that *love is truth*, then truth itself must be painful! Now you've proven that pain and loss have occurred in the past, which, when felt in the present, serves to keep you from letting go to love in the *now*. This is ridiculous, of course. I don't know much, but I do know that if we cannot trust truth (love) there is no hope for anyone. But of course, the truth is true, and, of course, it is upholding and loving.

*Just remember that anything from the past
that does not feel peaceful was false then, so
it must be now!*

Using this principle, we are now free from having to account for the past, refer to it, or revitalize it in the present. It can remain buried where it is . . . *nowhere*. Now, we can take a look at the original question: "Where does guilt come from?" Well, do you see it yet?

It comes from here and now.

*If only the "now" is experienced, then it
must be that all thoughts, points of view,
positions held, and choices are **currently**
chosen by the experiencer in the present.
In other words, we choose pain, loss, fear,
regret, grievance, victimhood, attack,
defense, littleness, and stuckness right now,
voluntarily, even though they seem to be
framed in the past.*

When we really get hold of this, our true power comes into view. We choose everything—the pain *and* the love, right here and now. We write the script, play the parts, and then critique our performances as either guilty or deserving. In each moment, we choose guilt or love, heaven or hell, conflict or peace. So who needs the past for guilt . . . there's plenty right here.

*Be careful not to slip away from this
point (that guilt is chosen in the present);
otherwise, you may find yourself continuing
to revert back to your past storyline and find
proof of yours or someone else's "guilt"
all over again.*

Sin: What a Bunch of *B.S.*!

That's perhaps the most freeing hook you can hang
your comfort on. Sin, as taken literally, is an old ar-
chery term that means "missing the mark" or error. We
can't stress this enough. Sin is error, and nothing more.
Sin is a simple mistake, part of an essential learning experience, which cannot hurt you or anyone else. How
does anybody learn anything if not by constant *doing?*
Of course, this *doing* is not always of clarity or knowl-
edge, nor does it always make sense. Fortunately, errors are eventually seen as nonproductive, as they play
out in relationships and situations that bring about unwanted results. It can be a fistfight resulting from insult
on the highway, or selfish behavior within a committed
relationship that brings about its demise, and/or everything in between. But one thing is for sure; without
the benefit of direct learning from mistakes, there *is no
learning at all.*

What kind of nonsense would it be to expect you to
know how to live, how to act, what choices to make in
all situations, when to give, when to take, or when to
stop giving, etc.? What are we supposed to do . . . come
to earth, from the start, as experts on life? Of course

not. Learning, then, in all forms, requires making errors as an integral part of growth. "Sin" (gratefully) accurately refers to those mistakes and events that point us toward truth and appropriateness . . . **but it *never* points to guilt; never, never, never.**

Why *Would* We Choose Guilt, Right Here and Now?

This is a strange but necessary question and, if we look closely, there is a twist. To choose guilt is ridiculous; we can all agree to that. In fact, I don't really know anyone who would do that voluntarily. That would mean one would seek out punishment consciously and agree to the penalty. But why would we do that? *Is* there a penalty buzzer inside that you can push, a lever you can pull . . . what's the process for guilt or punishment that is so automatic? We're "nuts" and it just happens by itself . . . could that be it? No.

> *It's not that you are choosing guilt —*
> *it's that you are **not** choosing love.*

In every moment of life, you have only to realize your own perfection and, then, actually feel it. It will feel relaxed in your tummy, in your chest, behind your eyes, and down to your extremities. Love always brings relaxation. Self-love, then, is the answer to guilt. *But* it must be chosen over and over. The only purpose for being able to choose anything, then, is to experience the immediate aftereffects of

the choice to self-love. This *feels* like being loved. It is unmistakable in that it feels like every*one* and every*thing* loves you . . . especially *you* for a change. I cannot stress this point enough.

The only purpose in choosing . . . is to choose Love.

This is a brilliant gift, in that you have now joined with Creation or God (however you see that) in the ongoing extension of the infinite. Everything extends— denial, acceptance, attack, forgiveness, clarity, obstacles, withholding and love. Choose for love, and you are participating in the most creative endeavor humanity has ever known. Be part of the solution to guilt and fear . . . *be* the solution!

I recently counseled a woman on this very subject. I asked her, "Are you able to love yourself now? Are you able to see yourself as lovable right now?"

She answered, "Yes, I am."

I was not convinced, however. She was saying the words, but I didn't have the sense that she really meant them. I rephrased my question: *"Are you willing to feel loved, right now?"*

She paused for a moment and said, "I guess not." That said it all. Conceptually, she was willing. Philosophically, she was in agreement with the principle. But in actuality, she was still unwilling to feel love, to feel lovable, to feel entitled to peace. Perhaps, by the time this book is published, she will have come around to another choice, one that instinctively enters the experience of wellness and deservitude.

Try it now: Say to yourself,

I am the perfect expression of happiness.
I am the love that I seek.
There are no restraints upon me, nor can there be.
I choose to feel loved, now.

You may have just discovered some unrealized resistance to love. You may feel nothing, or possibly some anxiety, as you invite love in. One thing is for sure; something will be revealed to you. It's not possible to ask a question or make a request and not be answered. Life doesn't work that way. It's not like you're on a mountaintop, your words getting lost in the elements. It's not empty space you are speaking with, it is life itself—it's Love, and it will never disappoint you. Most importantly, though, burn it into your mind that to NOT choose to feel loved allows guilt to reclaim your energy. Close the screen door, keep the flies out; choose for peace, and guilt will stay away. Choosing for love keeps the guilt-flies out. Love *is* a most effective "guilt spray!"

Why Do We Resist Feeling Loved?

Because we've got it backwards: what we believe is false, and what we deny is true.

Deep inside, we understand that if we are worthy of love, of feeling loved, everyone else must be, too. This presents a big problem for the ego. Bugs are bugs, birds are birds, beasts are beasts, and people are people — there are certain commonalities that we share. You know that old expression, "if it walks like a duck, etc." Well, if it walks on two legs and acts like a self-depre-cating "a-hole," then it's a human. We all cry, laugh, love to eat good food, love a "roll in the hay." BUT, when the chips are down, we don't trust many others. We're all guilty, and we know it.

Humanity shares many things, but most of all we share guilt. Guilt, then, is "presumed" to be our nor-mal internal state. The acceptance of guilt as an innate part of our being results in our expectation of attack or punishment from others. Hence, the ego sees the world as ruthless and dangerous. Others will try to defend themselves at our expense. This can come in the form of overt anger, criticism, blame, and insult as well as disingenuous pandering or manipulative "kindness." Naturally, the ego is comfortable with this game. We all use the rules of survival, and, to some extent, it *is* a level playing field since we can all be vicious. On the other hand, if I become accepting of another reality — the lov-ing honor that lies within —

then I must see this love and honor within
you as well.

Now my ego has a problem. How will I survive in a treacherous world where guilt and manipulation rule, and expect to survive with a lot of "sweet talk" from my insides as my only weapon? From this point of view, love *is* dangerous. The best defense, then, is to keep things as they are. *OK, I'm guilty, that's true, but so are you, which gives me the right to continue the same shtick.* I'll find a way to project my guilt upon you (and away from me) in order to feel good enough to sleep at night, and, when necessary, I'll defend myself against you. But at least I can feel justified in doing so since, after all, you *could* and *do* attack me as well. Out goes the baby with the bathwater, and so much for lofty ideas of innocence, self-love, and all the rest. Guilt has proven its worth; it is *safe(?)*.

But wait a minute . . . love is always appropriate . . . remember? And if you are willing to trust that and give it a chance to redefine "you," your upside-down world is suddenly righted. When Love is set loose to work its miracles, you cannot resist the peaceful inner feeling that takes over, replacing the fear, defensiveness, and anger. And it's so easy to do; just sit and breathe a moment, ask for guidance, and let Love solve the problem.

It never fails. Love cannot fail.

Self-Love —
Do I Really Deserve This?

Please, remember this, since we just can't say it enough: *All love is self-love.* All love is perfect love. All love is *completely* perfect. Therefore, *your* love is perfectly perfect.

If there were anything I could bring about, it would be your agreement that what you see in the mirror is all loving, all good, and all deserving. I know it's difficult to accept when the nightly news shows the latest child molestation, but using your new understanding that anything that is *not the expression of love* is the acting out of fear, you too will find a way to include the "molester" in your understanding of love.

Even if you find "god" mentality unacceptable, your love will still stand. Just your desire to feel loved should tell you something. Isn't that fascinating? No matter how absurd we act, how unsightly our behaviors and thoughts, how "stupid" we feel, our eternal longing to feel loved never changes. It is the only constant in a morass of conflict, violence, calm, happiness, sadness, sleep, or awakenness . . . that completely familiar need to feel cared about is always there. And it is *only* this desire that you'll ever need to establish your perfection. Perfect love loves perfectly. Perfect love desires only it*Self* to be felt.

Look at it this way:

> When you're hungry, do you question
> whether or not you're a being that requires
> food and drink?

> When you're tired, do you doubt that sleep is
> appropriate for you?

Of course you don't. So when you desire to feel loved, why question whether or not you "deserve" it? How silly. Love is your truth. Love is your home. Love is your desire. *Love is you.*

God, I love this stuff, don't you? To keep this fresh in your mind, constantly remind yourself that any thoughts, words, or actions that appear unloving or guilty are just acting out your belief that you are defective, nothing more. Imagine — no matter what you've thought, done, not done, felt, not felt, said, not said, denied, or caused . . . you are perfect love and that's that. There's not a damned thing you can do about it so you might as well buy it, hook, line, and sinker. You're all right, so it's time to lighten up about your life and the lives of all those around you. This is not an option and is not up for discussion. Accept it, and everything will change.

The Real Purpose of Behavior

*What you do and say tells you what you are
thinking and believing.*

There is no other purpose that behaviors will serve (other than to communicate love, and that will always be obvious). Everything you think, do, and say, then, is designed to let you know what's deep in your core-belief. Actions, thoughts, and conveyances are the end result of beliefs brought into visibility, nothing more. If you believe that life is dangerous, you will live defensively and be on guard, with all your hot buttons ready for action. This is how most of us live until we learn there *is* a better way.

Think of how extraordinary life would be if you always understood what someone was *really* trying to say or do. What would it be like if you were to experience unkindness from another and know that it was just a fearful person speaking . . . not a *bad* person? At least now you have a shot at helping to calm down that person by giving what's needed — a kind word or an understanding nod. Let's face it, though, most of the time we re-interpret someone else's struggle as an attack upon ourselves, bringing up our own fear and protection. That's all the ego needs to get going; they fired the first shot, so we make sure to fire the last. But again . . . if we accept that all utterances speak only of love or fear, then everyone deserves a pass all the time. That's how we learn . . . by recognizing what's born in fear, and then *unlearning* useless old responses.

Let's say someone acts or speaks unkindly or judgmentally of you. You carp back with your own "stuff," and the misunderstanding intensifies. Just as your neighbor misspoke from fear, so did you. But you're both still innocent. No matter how nasty this fight becomes, nothing ever really changes. The only problem is a perceived one. All you have to do is remember that nothing of substance happened at all, and you're both absolved from whatever was said, still perfect and unscathed as created. It always makes sense to take a look at every disturbing exchange, in order to learn how you could have reacted differently. That's how learning of any kind occurs, a little at a time in small doses we can handle.

When was the last time you could have been kinder to one who was struggling with something or other? Probably, within the past day or two! Take a look, see your own fear, forgive it, experience perfect innocence, then see the same innocence in your brother, sister, spouse, friend, or neighbor, and agree to act differently next time. Cause and effect at work in its truest form . . . acting, seeing, learning, choosing differently, feeling peaceful, and being filled with gratitude. This is the only purpose of life in the physical world—to grow wise and completely aware of universal innocence, starting with your own. This is not to say that inappropriate or abusive treatment need be tolerated. Just know that it's born in fear—not evil—and therefore is, in fact, harmless. This way, you can separate the behavior from the person; now no one has to be condemned.

The guiltless can free the fearful.

The Agreement to *Be* Love Makes Your Behavior Loving

Have you ever heard the expression "Don't change"? Sure you have. Well, that's usually said in jest but, here, *we really mean it*. The point is that if you try to act lovingly so that you deserve love, you'll be faking it. That never works, so don't bother.

But here's what does work: Accept that you are already completely loving in spite of what you've said or done up until now, and your healing has been set in motion. This principle is failsafe because all of your unwanted behaviors stem from your sense of guilt, which is always unreal. No matter what you've done, you are guiltless. As undeserved as it may feel, please believe this silly axiom: Kittens come from cats, puppies from dogs, and perfect love from perfect love. So, from your insistence that you are *only* love will come the kinds of words and deeds that will best represent that reality. For the first time in your life, you will be "acting" authentically, in that the part you are playing is who you actually are. No "B.S." here, my friends; for once, your love will accurately represent you in person.

Through your willingness to first be love
itself, you will re-establish the way you
interact with the world, thus
transforming your life from guilt
to innocence . . . from fear to love.

Now we're on to something. *From* your love will come your love. *From* your clarity and patience will come the same. All those in your life will grow from your example, and healing will spring forth from you like the scent from a flower. And the best part is that you don't have to work at it; your behavior will only be expressing your lovability . . . *not causing it.*

Vigilance in the Self-Loving Process

How do we know whether or not we're happy? It's sad, but you wouldn't believe the number of people who don't know how they feel . . . what a bizarre commentary on the human condition. It brings up the question of whether or not we actually trust our own "insides" to tell us who we are and what's going on. Imagine that; we're the most evolved beings on the planet, and still we need to learn how to read our own insides.

Here's a good rule of thumb:

▶ If you feel good, deep inside—in your heart— then believe it, because happiness is *always* from the heart and cannot be missed.

▶ But, if your so-called happiness is being caused by *someone* or *something* outside of you, then we've got a problem. That's "conditional love," and it will disappear when the conditions change. This is the dangerous kind of love, since it's not love at all. Real love never changes; it is the only constant that exists.

True love . . .
is peaceful and doesn't "futurize" or plan. It doesn't need anything, want for anything, ask for anything, depend upon anything, or fear anything. It just sits there and feels wonderful.

Conditional love . . .
worries, scripts, defends, edits, and controls, since its stability comes from all the outside stuff. It always feels unstable and can never be mistaken for peace because your mind is very aware that conditions could change in a heartbeat, making happiness unstable, and "poof" . . . we're back in distress.

So, if you feel the slightest bit uncomfortable, there is fear within, and you *do* believe that loss is coming. It can be nothing else. It's either love or fear of loss all the time . . . there are no other possibilities. Here's a simple formula for relief:

▶ Sit a moment and breathe.

▶ If you feel unrest or the need for protection of any kind, you're in fear (guilt).

▶ Now, go within and reacquaint yourself with the innocence you deserve.

▶ Feel the peace pouring into your body as your love **embraces** *itself*.

You might say, "Yeah, that's easy to say, but just how do I get from fear to feeling peace?" And I say to you, "Just do it!" (Example: you're at the edge of the pool. "Come on in," they say. Do you say, "How?" NO. You just do it; you jump. It's the same with feeling peace or love . . . you just do it.)

Try it now. Sit back right now and feel peace . . . see, you can!

Nobility

Nobility is a beautiful word when actualized. Nobility is the pure state of correctness and purity of intent.

Nobility is established by the being that experiences it.
All subsequent events are only reflections of that.

If you're anything like me, you always thought that only the "special ones" were deserving of the term "nobility." Somehow, some were just born into it, but certainly we couldn't expect to be that ourselves. Wrong. That is exactly what we're supposed to feel and believe. Our courage to assume nobility is "Christlike," in that nothing but perfection itself is truly noble . . . *nothing but you, in fact.*

Noble does as noble is. **The best way for you to change the way you move through the world is to accept your deservitude from this moment on, and cut the guilt crap.** Nobility is reserved for everyone, but, until we get that, we'll always see someone, some-where, as more deserving than we are. What could be easier than to ask the perfect being to accept himself? And what a lovely gift to bestow upon yourself and oth-ers. Jesus was noble. Buddha was noble. Joan of Arc was noble. Mother Teresa was noble. Your mom was/is noble, along with her children!

I always get a kick out of how willing we are to see the innocence and perfection of a newly born baby. How lovely to be in the presence of such a miracle, and how noble to give birth. But what happens to that perfectly innocent newborn? It "morphs" into a guilty, savage, judgmental creep that deserves to be punished. Can you see how nonsensical this is? And what about Mom . . . if the newborn is innocent and perfect, why wouldn't it be a perfect replication of where it came from — Mom, of course . . . so Mom must have been perfect too.

The natural laws of extension demand that what comes from something (the effect) is never unlike what it comes from (its cause). From Creation (whatever that is) comes the perfectly created. Therefore, what comes from you is nothing more than a perfect expres-sion of how you're willing to see yourself. See yourself as perfect, and all expressions will be noble in nature. Say it to yourself in the mirror tonight while brushing your teeth:

> I am noble.
> I am perfect love.
> I am here to learn of my deservitude.

Here's another way to see your own nobility. You're at the zoo, and among the animals is a regal-looking lion . . . at peace, just sitting and looking, and definitely in charge. You could say, "What a noble animal," and you'd be right. But the nobility you felt in that moment came from you, not the animal. It was from your own mind that the experience and understanding of nobility arose; it was *your* nobility being triggered by the lion.

My mind is limitless.
The power of my love is limitless.
My Cause and my effects are One.

Believe in Something . . . But Believe!

Most of what's wrong in the world today is caused by distorted and painful self-images. We see the world through our own self-deprecating eyes, and no one is freed from the traction of our own bondage. What you see, you project, and what you project, you believe. So if you don't like what you've been seeing lately, it's time to believe in something else.

Remember that great song, "Do You Believe in Magic"? Well, how about this: Are you willing to believe in love, truth, honor, and innocence? Are you willing to see it in your own eyes, looking back into your own soul? If you do, your innermost dreams of happiness are about to be realized.

Beliefs can change your life forever.
Beliefs control the universe . . . your universe.

Let's agree that we all believe in something. It doesn't matter whether it's God or nature, intelligent design or happenstance. Just add your willingness to believe that there is true purpose to your life, and you will have established the agenda that brings you "home." You've heard that expression "home." It means back to your true Self, where only peace resides. If there is any purpose to anything, it's to establish the reality of peace within.

What other purpose could there be for the potential to feel peace other than to feel it?

When you are at peace, there is no conflict. When you are at peace, you have chosen to accept that natural state of joy that will always embrace you. Belief in peace removes all opposing potentials so that unity and wholeness are seen everywhere, even in past appearances of conflict. Trust this, and freedom is yours. Trust your mind-power, and watch your life rearrange itself before your loving eyes.

Your inner voice was made for you.

The language of your own inner voice will always adjust itself to accommodate what you need at the time. It's not possible that inner guidance is offered in ways that are not comfortably felt. That's the beauty of "guidance"—it always knows exactly what you need to see in order to help you become free.

That expression, "You'll know what to do, where to go, what to say and to whom" from *ACIM* is not a joke.

It's completely true. The trouble is, we don't often believe in that soft inner voice. Just as I have asked you
to believe in something—anything—why not choose to
believe in your own celestial guidance deep inside about
any issue, relationship, action, inclination, boundary,
choice, and everything else? The essence of your very
being is softly speaking all the time.

It knows everything you need to know, right now.

▶ It knows what's right and what's wrong.

▶ It knows what's best for you in any situation.

▶ It knows how to handle fear.

▶ It is uncompromisingly honest.

▶ It is your love in the purest form.

But deny it, and you deny yourself what you've
always wanted . . . your own voice in the world. The
funny thing is that the world *needs* to hear your voice.
We all can learn from what you have to say and how
you say it. When you're speaking from that honorable
place deep inside, you will never be doubted or misunderstood, and we out in your world will always benefit
and learn from your connection to Self. There is nothing else that is authentic nor is there anything else that
could possibly be of service to us.

Your Voice is everything.
Your denial of Self renders an empty landscape,
dead and cold.

So please, along with my asking you to believe in something, believe in that perfect guide in your core, that reliable soft influence always offering the very best *to one who will listen.*

Don't Worry; You Are *Not* Alone

Whenever I'm in front of an audience at a meeting or workshop, I am blessed by how connected I feel to everyone I see. But as people speak and interact, I'm astounded at how separate *they* feel. So I make it a point to remind folks that we are all feeling the same things most of the time. We all want to feel loved, included, understood, respected and safe, but we still fear that something we do or say will reveal our guilt.

But how we act in any given moment is always determined by how connected or disconnected we are to our own insides. The less connected, the more protected and distant our demeanor. The more connected, the more open and available we are to each other.

We all experience the same phenomenon . . . we are identical in this regard.

If you are uncertain about your own worth and feel the guilt of your past or present experiences, you will try to hide these dirty little secrets, and phony up some personality to get you through the moment. No wonder you are afraid . . . it's very alone in that place. We've all felt it, and it's awful . . . that hideaway inside; that's where we hide our "guilt."

Inevitably, though, through the course of an evening almost everyone will eventually connect to the group experience and become visible and honest. It's so beautiful to watch people relaxing into commonality. And, once that happens, the guilt evaporates and everything changes. A frightened self-conscious man will laugh and let his charm really show; a woman suffering with a poor self-image will say, "What the hell . . ." and let go with what's really on her mind. Suddenly, the room becomes alive with enthusiasm as people authentically interact with the innocence they really are. In this setting, fear disappears, differences evaporate, *and nobody feels alone*. It *is* magic, and we're the magicians! So let's forget about this business of being alone . . . we're never alone and that's that. Whatever you're thinking, we've thought it too. Isn't it great to be the same?!

Commitment!

I always have to laugh in my office or at a gathering when I ask someone who is working through his or her issues, "Well, are you ready now? Are you committed to this new way of thinking (guiltless)?"

And they say, "I'm working on that," or "I think so," or "Yeah, that's what I have to do."

"Right," I say. "But, are you really?"

"Well, I think so, that's what I'm here for, isn't it?"

That's a flabby, half-hearted agreement to allow change if I ever heard one. From that weak focus can come no useful clues to a better life. The refusal to commit is actually the refusal to let go of the current m.o., which, of course, is designed to keep us safe in the guilty world we know. If nothing changes, nothing changes; without letting go of the old, the new cannot arrive.

When the mind is filled with fearful, defensive, and judgmental behaviors, there's no room for an inchworm to wriggle in, never mind a whole different way of seeing yourself.

Commitment means a choice has been made to welcome the remedy for an old problem. And if we believe that we deserve to feel renewed and are capable of learning how to feel directed from a loving influence that only has our best interests at heart, the message will get in and everything unwanted will disappear. This leads to fulfillment on many levels. We've all seen the teachers of abundance bombarding the media with the solutions to poverty and stuckness. You know who they are and what they're saying: "Trust yourself."

"Believe that you can do it. Accept that you deserve it. Now, buy these CDs and do it!"

The truth is, they're right. A simple commitment *will* carve out a space a day at a time for growth and progress at a rate most comfortable for you. Healing will never ask you to feel pain or to lose your sense of self.

Progress is measured in how good you feel,
not in how fast you change.

There is another aspect to this commitment issue that needs revealing here. Unfortunately, we often stick to the old script as a form of defiance against anyone or anything that might be asking us to change. I have clients who do that with food. His/her eating is addictive in nature. They will eat belligerently which maintains an unhealthy body image, and keeps the focus off of their real problems—*guilt and fear.* As long as the focus is on food (it's too obvious to miss), the other issues are never brought to the table. It's too filled with food!

Check your own life now and see if there are some persistent behaviors that eclipse the real self-image issues which, when revealed, can be corrected with the slightest commitment. Commitment, then, is a statement of uncompromising honesty that will help us come clean and face the music about our inner struggles.

Commitment will bring you everything
you thought impossible.

Can't or Won't . . . That Is the Question

Shakespeare said, "To be or not to be, that is the question." "To be" means to be in the here and now with empowerment, creativity, and spirit. That means *you can.* "Not to be" means you're disabled by some mysterious demon from the outside, and *you can't.* But if that's true, then all of your choices, impulses, proclivities and feelings are happening *to* you and are not coming *from* you . . . now we're back to the same old problem. Can you imagine what a travesty life would be if you really had no *say*? I can't think of a hell worse than that.

I have a dear old friend who comes to see me from time to time. Invariably, the subject of believing or commitment to something—anything—comes up. He waxes through his repertoire of stuckness and, with assurance, restates that he just can't seem to be able to commit or believe. No matter how hard he tries, *he just can't do it.*

Hogwash. He can do anything he wants to do . . . but underneath where the frightened little ego is hiding, the thought of having to surrender all the defenses and weapons to something you can't see or touch, such as "belief or faith," is asking too much. As we know, the ego is very smart. It literally lives to live. Its primary assignment is to survive, and what could be more threatening to a frightened ego than a minefield full of commitment to truth, honesty, defenselessness, unconditional giving, love, and visibility? To the ego, this means death. To commit asks that we let go of all fear-based living principles and trust the guidance from a deeper place inside . . . not from the little hiding place in which the ego resides.

So, I can't? You *can't?* How about you and I agree to never say that again? From now on, we can!

The new question is, "*Will* we?"

Will we agree to these new terms for living peacefully? If I agree that I can bring about whatever mind-set I choose, then remaining stuck is unnecessary. Here is where the rubber meets the road. Since we have agreed to become honest about it and admit that change is optional and not controlled from the outside, refusing new possibilities becomes an "I won't," not an "I can't." If nothing is changing, you have disallowed anything new to enter your tightly protected little world. It's not that you couldn't . . . you wouldn't. Just by admitting this, we've taken a definite step up from "I can't."

- *"I can't"* means you're helpless, and it is a kind of death.

- *"I won't"* acknowledges that you do have the power, and that brings hope.

- *Hope* is a statement of faith . . . and, suddenly, **a light goes on.**

Seeing this dug-in position of "I can't" is important, since the willingness to look always brings about empowerment. By admitting our part in the stuckness, the door swings open and welcomes in that loving inner guide who is always standing just outside, waiting for our invitation.

Do this tonight just before you go to bed. Whisper softly to yourself:

I can. I will. It is done.

Then go to sleep and see what happens. You can do anything you want to do, including experience the beauty of your own guidance **that needs only your faith in it** to bring about a new life.

I can . . . I will . . . it is done.

Jump!

This morning was a perfect example for me. I woke up feeling shaky and a little down. I started thinking about all the things that needed doing, especially finishing this book. As I lay there in bed, I felt the resistance. There I was, all caught up in my own storyline of obstacles and challenges. I was just plain stuck.

Then I remembered that beautiful sentiment from *A Course In Miracles*. It's not a direct quote, but it basically asks that we "go toward what we're afraid of."

> If you're afraid to call a certain person, call them now.
>
> If you're avoiding taking care of a nagging tax problem, do it now.
>
> Whenever you are avoiding anything, it's fear . . . one problem . . . one solution.
>
> Don't think — *jump*!

I "jumped" this morning and, so far, I've had a great day. It's not that I made any great discoveries, or that someone dropped off a check; it's that when I'm willing to jump into what I've been avoiding, the emptiness of my fear is revealed. And after just a few seconds without the crippling effects of fear in my face, I'm able to remember the truth: I am innocent, deserving, entitled, and guaranteed peace just by showing up. It doesn't get any easier than that. Don't worry about how you're going to fix something or solve something; just put yourself there, right in the middle of it and watch what happens. You'll always know what to do—sometimes not until you actually do it, but that's all right too.

It's the nature of truth to not plan,
but to allow solutions to unfold in their own way.

This does require an ironclad faith, however. So let's agree that just your "jumping in" is immediately an outward expression of your faith. Just the other day, I heard a wise man offer some good advice about faith. He said, **"Feed your faith, and starve your doubts to death."** I plan to remember that every day. This brings us the real power, the kind that never lets you down.

Healing Is Continuous

To feel guiltless and free today requires a conscious re-membering that you *are*.

Although your actual guiltless self is quite safe and sound without any effort at all, you don't necessarily believe that. So you can *feel* guilty and fearful moment after moment, sometimes day after day, unless you take action to undo the old bad habits.

Here on Cape Ann in Massachusetts, it's been raining for eight days now, and we're told it will contin-ue another three or four. But inside, we're warm and dry—not because we have no leaks—but because the sump pump is churning away every five minutes re-moving the invading water.

Guilt and fear require the same vigilance; when they show up, you must dump them. Self-doubt and a host of other depressing thoughts are constantly pressing in on your consciousness saying you need to remain protected and hidden. And every time you take the bait, they've won. Doesn't it feel terrible to wake up that way . . . and then have to struggle through the day with that monkey on your back?

But as we've said, you (the chooser) can *remember to remember* that:

You are complete, healed, and whole, shining in the reflection of love. In you, threat is impossible, love is perfected, and joy is established without opposite. You are the home of love itself. You are the heaven where this love resides. You are sinless and, in your purity lies the truth of all creation.

(Content from ACIM)

All this you can have in a heartbeat just by an ongoing agreement to heal now, to heal again, and again and again.

At first, it can feel strange. I remember walking around like an old drunk (I'm sober now for twenty years by the grace of God) mumbling to myself, "I'm OK. I'm not guilty. I deserve to be happy. Yes, I'm in the right place, right now. I'm innocent." God knows how many people saw me and wondered who the hell I was talking to, but who cares; it worked then and it still works today.

Love is an inside job;
it comes from inside and winds up there.

So keep the invitations coming; literally, invite your entitlement to feeling good into your mind-set and let the amazing effects of truth and love have their way with you today.

I'm OK, You're OK— That's No Joke!

The guiltless have a job to do. We're all in this together and we know it. When you have the gift of feeling deserving and free, you must give it away. And the best way to do that is to see your neighbor the same way: guiltless and deserving. Whatever we bring into our consciousness is always shared in every relationship. It doesn't matter how casual or intimate the relationship is, your current internal barometer is visible for all to see. If you feel wonderful, they will know, and, not only that, they will feel better just being around you. Have you ever noticed how a kind word or a tussle of your hair gives you a lift? Well, that's what we do for each other when we finally wake up and see our guiltlessness.

People who are just plain down come to see me all the time. When they leave, they're usually smiling. Invariably, they will say, "Gee, I feel so much better, etc."

So what happens in those magical sessions in my office that changes the way folks feel? Can you guess? Yes, I share with my clients *my* gratitude and vision. I share the vision of my own innocence and deservitude, and the expectation of good things. I share that we are the same, and what's true for me is true for them. I ask them to trust the simple truth that their love means everything, and that nothing else does. I hold a vision of wellness for them until they are willing to move into it personally. That's my job, and it works.

It has to be true, this healing message . . . it's all about the mind and what we do with it. I can make heaven or hell right now according to how my intention is set. Aim left, and I'll hit the barn door; aim right, the fire hydrant. But if I'm standing upright so I can see the target clearly, I'll hit the bull's eye—the one in my heart. Yes, Dear Ones, aim for the heart, and you will bring many along with you; and they will also learn how to "dump the junk" and awaken to guiltlessness.

So, that's the deal. We all share this assignment. Let's take it on with certainty of purpose and bring the light to anyone who needs what you have. Give it away, and then hold on to your seatbelts. Remember . . . the truth intensifies as it is shared!

Old Habits Are Persistent

You're darn right they are. If you want to prove it, just pay attention to what you do, think and feel in the next hour. Whatever it is, will be a recreation of the last time you had the same experience. *Everything* is a "repeat" of yesterday's movie until you go into a different theater . . . a different program deep in your mind where the context of all meaning is chosen. Let's remember that all thoughts and feelings are the effects of beliefs already in place, which, once again, have been called upon to verify themselves on the surface through behaviors and feelings. These are the voices for guilt, defect, and fear. Simon and Garfunkel might as well have sung, "Still *GUILTY* after all these years!"

Once in motion, these old habits *remain* in motion until purposefully changed or modified. How many times have you said about somebody, "They'll never change," or about yourself, "I always do this . . . I hate that about me"? These repetitive methods have cut a "groove" into your behaviors and have their own course. Watch yourself for a few minutes today, and see how you react to people and events without even thinking. Before you know it, you respond with judgments, anger, laughter, fear, or joy (depending on how safe you feel). The point is that guilt is firmly entrenched in the mind-set and serves to go off every hour like "Old Faithful" unless we take action.

I recommend a humble request to your honorable Inner Guide for something new, trusting and nonmanipulative. Your request will be granted, and everything *will* be new. Maybe you won't overreact and be so defensive, and maybe you don't have to know all the answers right now—you *can* choose a different path that easily. For once, just listen and allow yourself a few minutes to understand what's needed or offered by another. Or, when by yourself in those moments of stuckness, see how you can be magically lifted out of the muck into new possibilities that would ordinarily be blocked by the old fear-driven responses.

ACIM has, among many brilliant daily exercises, one that says, "I could see peace instead of this." When accepted even for an instant, just that momentary confirmation of your ability to choose differently makes its mark upon your soul and, at once, the old persistent responses are disallowed, carving a new groove for innocence and deservitude.

The more you do it, the stronger it gets. The stronger it gets, the more you trust it. The more you trust it, *the more you do it.* Eventually, *it* becomes the new protocol, and the old fearful ways can be put to rest. There's no trick or special talent necessary for making these positive changes deep within . . . only your willingness to remember to choose again.

*You can ask now for guidance to lead the
way through today, and it is done.*

*Your innocence is always ready to speak on
your behalf . . . when invited.*

The Power of *Your* Love Can Do Anything

No truer words were ever said. Not only *can* it do anything, but it will literally reinvent you, bring you abundance, and propel you all the way to the awakened state. Our only job is to let it. I wish there were some way to prove this on paper, but there isn't. It will be proven, though, by your willingness to give Love the reins and let it fly.

Many years ago, I was brought in as a consultant to a modest record label in order to assist in the recording, mixing, and mastering of the company's (then) limited artist roster. The more I got involved, the more it became clear to me that none of the principal owners had much musical talent themselves. They knew what they liked, but that was it. There was no natural production talent, engineering ability, or familiarity with the language of music. I've often marveled at what actually happened to them over the years. They exploded into a huge conglomerate, an extremely visible worldwide label with many well-known recording stars. So, how did that happen?

There is one ingredient they *did* have . . . they all three shared the same vision. They *loved* the music, believed in the artists, and worked hard. It wasn't talent that put them on the map; it was pure dedication. It was their spirit that did the job. There are thousands of stories like this one—endless numbers of successful happy people just following their hearts and allowing the rest to happen by itself. You can do the same with *your* love; trust it, and it will lead you through the guilt/stuckness battle to peace of mind and clarity in your life. Deny it, and, in ten years, you will be exactly where you are today.

The power of Love will deny guilt,
push through hardship, and create limitlessly.

From Guilt to Euphoria

I know euphoria sounds ridiculous, but listen to this story. Forty-five years ago, I was in the military and stationed in Germany on a little security base. We were a strange bunch. Most were college grads (I wasn't) and smart.

One day, during an odd conversation with my room-mate, I looked at him, took aim, and fired my most devastating hateful shot. I said, "You know what I'd like to do, Dave? I'd like to find someone, learn everything they can do, and then *do it better right in front of them.*"

He looked at me with inquisitive eyes and said, "You're either crazy or sick, my friend. That's the meanest thing I ever need to hear from another human being." When we were discharged, we went our separate ways. He never got over that remark, and our friendship ended.

Until recently, I've tried to push that "guilty event" out of my mind, often several times a month. Still, inside, it remained as vivid as ever. Then, my friend Teresa gave me a movie called, *The Five People You Meet in*

Heaven. It was a little slow and disjointed, but there were scenes from a character's early life involving the military and some tough moments that changed the course of his life. This got me thinking . . . and . . . something monumental happened. I got the answer. I saw myself back in the barracks with my roommate, Dave, and felt myself saying that awful thing to him.

Quietly, during the movie, I asked myself, "Why did you say that, John? . . . that you'd like to find someone, learn everything they can do, and then *do it better right in front of them."*

And then it came, as gently as a snowflake. The Voice said,

> *"Because you felt at the time that anything*
> ***you*** *would ever do, someone else would*
> *always do better, so why try anything at all?*
> *It was about you, John, all about YOU."*

Yes, that was it! That was the answer. All these years, I felt corrupt and guilty that I could even think such an evil thought — and all the time it was my own fear of being inadequate and outdone by everyone else.

I can't tell you how incredible that moment was for me. Not only did it free me completely from being a diabolical a-hole, but it explained why I never followed my heart into several careers that I often dreamed about. Think of it . . . decades of pain and guilt removed and understood in a heartbeat. I wasn't guilty of meanness, but I was convinced that my insides were insufficient, lacking, and, of course, guilty, so why would *I* ever succeed at anything?

Just in these past few days, that one moment has changed my life immensely. Here, at almost the end of this book, a new guiltless "me" is emerging. You can have this too, just by looking at yourself with kind eyes and knowing that your anger, resentments, and judgments are always about you, and not anyone else. Here lies the answer to every question you could ever have about the purpose of life itself:

It is to learn what you really believe;
it is to dispel the falsity, and finally discover
your innocent loving Self.

How beautiful the journey, and how fitting, that your love finds its way to the altar of truth where it can be shared with everyone. Remember, the truth is always shared; it's guilt that keeps to itself.

You see, whatever we think, say, or hide never actually speaks of our guilt (since we've agreed that we have none), **but only of our fear of *being* guilty.** Over and over you must say this until it "clicks in."

Euphoric? Yes, I am today. Thank you, God, and *you*, reader, for traveling with me down the long road to guiltlessness!

Stability . . . Who Will Protect Me?

It's a fair question and deserves an answer. Your ego wants some assurances that your entrance into a guiltless world won't turn you topsy-turvy and leave you disoriented. It wants guarantees that everything will remain stable. In short, the ego (your self-image of littleness) will accept change as long as nothing changes—of course, that's what the ego always wants. But there is a principle you can hang on to as you risk letting go of guilt. *And* it is very easy to understand; so easy that it's tempting to not take it seriously. But try it anyway. Believe with all your heart that:

Only fear (guilt) needs protection.
Love (innocence) fears nothing.

Choose to see yourself as perfect Love, and fear is gone.
Choose otherwise, and fear rules.

Be innocent, and you deserve peace. Be guilty, and you will bring about loss. In truth, it is not possible to fear loss of any kind when experiencing innocence. But you must be ready to buy that. I'm asking you to put the cart before the horse, to choose innocence without any guarantee that you will be safe in this experience without your defenses in full force. It takes some grit, but you can do it.

Deny defect, littleness, and guilt on every level, and you have chosen to acknowledge only the good, the deserving, the "real you." You'll know you've done it because it always feels good. In your acceptance of guilt, defect, and littleness there can be no peace, and this never feels good. That's how you know which choice you've made. This is why it's essential that you pay attention to your feelings; **they always speak according to your choices.**

Freedom

When you remove the crude material guilt-crust, your beauty is revealed. Challenges remain, problems still need solving, and taking responsibility becomes paramount. BUT, for once you can act with dignity and grace in dealing with life on life's terms without fear of reprisal, punishment, pain, humiliation, embarrassment, etc. Genuine honesty is the "out-picture" of innocence. You cannot miss it because it comes from the heart. Stability, then, is guaranteed from within and needs nothing from the outside to prop it up. This is real freedom in the truest sense.

Yours is the stability you seek.

The bottom line here is that whatever we feel that isn't warm, snuggly, and relaxed is always going to be fear . . . fear of something happening or something not happening, fear of being this or that, excluded, included, passed over, getting something we don't want, losing something we do want . . . but whatever it is, it's always fearful.

In the absence of fear, we are always relaxed, frivolous, and lighthearted. That's our natural state as with all things in nature. In the absence of anything that would aggravate a flower, the petals remain open. In the absence of anything upsetting to any animal, pet, person, fish, or bug, they are just fine and at rest. Peace, then, is the absence of fear because peace is the "being" experiencing itself without thought or protective radar, certainly *with* a sense of itself, but without any specific consciousness of being at peace. It simply *is* at peace, and is free.

Without peace, fear is. *Without* peace or love, there can be no freedom, since freedom is creative and flows from the heart. Fear disallows spontaneity and prevents your power from expressing itself. It will help to say this to yourself every morning:

> Fear binds — Love frees.
> Fear frightens — Love comforts.
> Fear is false — Love is true.

The Wisdom of Innocence

Innocence brings the ultimate comfort since, within its vision, **the complete emptiness of fear is revealed.** It expects to be happy. Innocence doesn't invite two possibilities—joy or pain. It doesn't entertain the idea of *two* identities. Innocence presumes only happiness because innocence is itself a statement of deservitude. It's not that deservitude is consciously experienced, as in "I deserve this therefore I demand it," but is instead the ultimate meaning of deservitude, which is the presumption of and the expectation of "happiness," which is the most creative potential we have. To expect happiness is to allow love to invite, to be invited, to extend, and to share . . . they're all the same. Love always extends and, therefore, is always inviting itself to love and to feel loved, quite literally agreeing to feel itself as it is. Innocence will expect, implement, and employ itself toward happiness, fulfillment, good humor, laughter, and creativity. It's the natural progression of things in the healthy state of mind.

When is the flower most magnificent? When its petals are open, while it's opening, or when the bud is forming? I don't know. The whole thing is mysterious and beautiful. The entire process of a flower coming from a plant, which comes from a shoot, which comes from a root system, which comes from a seed, *which comes from a flower* . . . is astounding. Love (innocence) is the same. Whether it's being expressed, received, invited, shared, or celebrated, it's no different from the flower phenomenon—just different aspects of the same thing. The whole phenomenon is beautiful, and, best of all, it's what you are!

Make It So

Let's agree, then, that innocence allows for nothing other than the expectation of fulfillment. And since it fears nothing, it must be the answer to those situations we find ourselves in where we expect to be demeaned or passed over; to lose, be ignored, or underrated; to be challenged or somehow competed against.

There's not a person reading this that hasn't grown up with some level of conviction that either there was something wrong inside that wasn't understood, or that they have been wronged somehow by something outside, since they have often times not felt appreciated. This formulates a foundation for the *ongoing expectation* for lack, disappointment, or defeatism.

I know of only one cure for this deadly disorder, and now you know it too: *Innocence.*

Innocence is the antidote. It is the healing influence, bringing itself into the presence of defect and guilt-feelings of any kind.

Be innocent and be free. Turn on the light and shine away fearful nonsense. Not to keep harping on the idea that guilt is the problem and innocence the answer, but if you invest your heart and soul into believing it, life becomes beautiful. Here's a way to keep it simple:

Guilt —demands that we must be careful. . . .
Pain is the result.
*Innocence — presumes that good times are
coming. . . .* **So they do.**

It's Easier Than Sleep

We all feel these two conditions, guilt and innocence, so it makes sense that we must remove one in order to embrace the other. A computer breaks down, and we pull out the hard drive and put in a new one. When the car sputters, we replace the carburetor. When it won't turn over, we change the starter motor. When our bodies go bad, we do the same thing. My wife is having a knee replaced; you get your teeth fixed. We do these things all the time. When parts of us don't work, we replace them.

Seeing things that way, the notion that our guilt-sense needs replacing with innocence becomes tenable. But it's even easier than that:

*We're asked to accept the reality of being
innocent without having to replace anything.
Just seeing ourselves as we are is sufficient.
The sense of guilt will fade away by itself.*

We've all heard fairytales about a commoner in some corner of the world who, out of the blue, learns that he's a prince! He's part of the kingdom now and "poof," he goes from nothing to everything. How long does it take for that fellow to grow into his new identity? *How long would it take you?* Not long, I'd say.

> "You mean, I'm not poor any more?
> OK, I can learn how to live this way . . .
> I know how to do this.
> I know how to be happy.
> I know how to have things;
> I can do this."

Well, it's no different with establishing innocence where guilt once reigned. It's not a matter of having to transform anything into something different, but just the allowance of the transformative *experience* deep within, which takes on the very character of innocence. The actuality of the being is *not* being altered at all. Our consciousness has been informed that what we thought was true—that we were guilty and poverty stricken in terms of our birthright—was just an error . . . nothing more. It's as though the mailman says,

> "Oh, you know what?
> I gave you the wrong papers; *these* are yours!
> *This* is the certificate of deservitude and
> innocence that was meant for you,
> not this guilt junk mail."

It's a diploma with a note saying, "You've graduated with honors!" And the "mailman" is your own love coming into awareness with the definitive guiltless message. It comes from you, to you, whenever you decide. This is all you will ever need to demonstrate your worth, your character, and your deservitude. The only question now is how long you will wait before taking what's yours. It's that easy. As *ACIM* says:

"Healing is easier than sleep."

Oh, But How We Can Resist It!

Do we forget to remember? Yes.
Does it take repetition to get this? Yes, it does.
But, is it easy? Yes.
Can anybody do it? Anyone can do it.

When you're hungry, do you need to be taught how to eat or do you just eat? When you're thirsty, you drink. When you're starving for a sense of acceptance and worth, allow it, and *it* will find you.

This is the most natural expression that the creative being is capable of—the acceptance of love, the presumption of love, the entitlement of love, the protection and safety of love. It is all a part of the divine consciousness you see in the mirror.

So if we say that all of those fears that support the need to hide in the background simply need to be understood as a slip of the metaphorical tongue, a misspeak, a little dream, a case of mistaken identity that's easily corrected which asks only for your acceptance of it, suddenly the transformation from hell to heaven becomes doable. Remember, innocence fears nothing, but does expect fulfillment. It doesn't think it up or control it — *it allows it.* It's like a telegram has come (anyone else here remember a telegram?) and is delivered to you, personally. It's saying,

> "Hello." Stop
> "We love you." Stop
> "No problem . . . just a big mistake." Stop
> "Have a ball." Stop
> Signed," The Universe." Stop

That's the message. And, what would *you* do? If you were with a friend, you'd yell out,

> "Hey, I got a telegram."
> "Oh yeah? What'd it say?"
> "Everything's fine!"
> "No shit."
> "Yeah; it was all just a . . . forget it, it's
> too complicated to explain. But trust me,
> everything's fine now."
> "That's great," your friend would say.

That's all we have to do. Innocence expects happiness, and it knows no fear. From now on, whenever you get caught up in the controlling and dramatizing of any event, and you feel discomfort inside — *you've just forgotten something.* So I guess it's time to send yourself a telegram.

I've just sent all of you a telegram, and
I truly hope you can feel it: Guiltless!

Celebrate vs. Overlook

This takes some practice. What we've discussed up until now is your vigilant commitment to Truth and Love. That is, your commitment to see Truth and Love from your own heart, and, subsequently, from the hearts of others. As we become more willing to take this on, naturally we'll look for evidence of our success. *You all know what's coming . . . don't you!* While you're busy monitoring your efforts to forgive, trust, and be fulfilled, you're also on guard for your "failure" to do so. Every time you forget and say a harsh word, condemn another in your mind, or lapse into fearful sadness or stuckness, you *will* notice. Your mind is all too willing to give as much meaning to its "failures" as it is to its successes. Now especially, it's essential that you keep in touch with how you interpret any thought or behavior.

A dear friend of mine and mentor for years, Tom Carpenter, recently reminded me of how subtle but powerful the attraction to guilt can be to your "judgmental mind." This "mind" is all too eager to find the same fault with your *Self* as it does with anyone else. When you make a mistake, the old condemning disbelieving voice for littleness gets very loud. And no matter what progress you have made, the case will still be made for your phony little attempts at love. **Now, it's time for your courage.**

Do you have the stones to celebrate your successes and overlook the screw-ups?

Because if you don't, guilt wins, time is wasted, and that lousy feeling is back. This goes against all that we have been taught throughout the ages, that we take the good with the bad. We can accept praise for our accomplishments, but we must take our medicine when we mess up. After all, "nobody's perfect," blah, blah, blah. But now, suddenly, you're asked to receive the praise, the love, and the comfort for remembering what's true, and to overlook (forgive) all errors of anger, judgment, or attack. It seems like we're getting a pass for unacceptable behavior . . . well, we are, and isn't that wonderful?

Love always teaches us to use every circumstance
for healing, not ever for punishment.

This literally means that when we make an error, we're asked to see the complete lack of content there and resume our innocence in the next moment. This renders all errors as having no residual effects, thus immediately insulating us from the negative effects of our mistakes.

Let me share this with you: Just the other day, there were several people visiting our home after a beautiful weekend workshop on healing led by old friends, Tom and Linda Carpenter. I was in the kitchen serving refreshments, making coffee, and talking with those in the other room (not paying too much attention to exactly what I was doing in the moment). I quickly reached into the fridge and grabbed a nonalcoholic beer (I'm sober now for twenty years) and said, "Gee, this tastes weird."

Of course, you know the rest. I was horrified . . . it was real beer . . . and I just "slipped!"

The next day, I shared my sad story with Tom. He looked at me, smiled, and said, "John; did you like it?"

"No," I said.

"Isn't that wonderful?" he asked. "You drank alcohol, it had no effect, and you had no inclination to continue . . . what a gift, you're healed!"

I can't tell you how deeply that affected my state of mind in just a few seconds. He was right. Just by using that experience to feel healed and freed from the insanity of alcohol, I could celebrate with gratitude and be free. But look how I was going down the other path of guilt and a breach of my sobriety. The point is that we must keep on our toes about how we interpret and use any and all experiences—to heal or to punish. Like anything else, this takes a little practice, but serves us to no end when deeply understood.

The Process

Everything is a learned process, which develops over the course of time with commitment and practice. When I became sober in AA, there wasn't much I understood, and what I did, came hard. Life in those days had mostly to do with getting what I wanted, *when* I wanted it, and I was certainly not used to trusting anything, especially patience, or "being just another Bozo on the bus." In fact, *I* wanted to be unique, high above all the other Bozos and, of course, this meant that I had special considerations. But with time and the patience of the wonderful AA support group, even I came to understand what commitment really means: It doesn't mean that you say "OK" and understand the program. It means that you say "OK" and *start* the gradual process of relearning what life is really about.

Whenever we are asked to embrace kindness, tolerance, forgiveness, laughter, empathy, humility, and the courage to change, we are building an internal empire that is the power of love in its purest form. This doesn't happen overnight, but it always does happen. Trust and try—believe and be patient with the only process that's really worth investing in. When you do, it will look like this!

Guilty, guilty, guilty, guilty, guilty, guilty, guilty, guilty, guilty, guilty, guilty, guilty, guilty, guilty, guilty, guilty, guilty, guilty, guilty.
Guilty, guilty, guilty, guilty, guilty, guilty, guilty, guilty, guiltless, guilty, guilty, guilty, guilty, guilty, guilty, guilty.
Guilty, guiltless, guilty, guilty, guilty, guilty, guilty, guilty, guiltless, guilty, guilty, guilty, guilty, guilty.
Guilty, guilty, guilty, guiltless, guilty, guilty, guilty, guiltless, guilty, guilty, guilty, guiltless.
Guiltless, guilty, guilty, guiltless, guilty, guilty, guilty, guiltless, guilty, guilty, guiltless.
Guiltless, guilty, guilty, guiltless, guilty, guiltless, guilty, guiltless, guilty.
Guiltless, guilty, guiltless, guiltless, guilty, guiltless, guilty, guilty.
Guiltless, guilty, guiltless, guiltless, guilty, guiltless, guilty, guiltless.
Guiltless, guilty, guiltless, guiltless, guiltless, guiltless.
Guiltless, Guiltless, Guiltless, Guiltless, Guiltless.
Guiltless, Guiltless, Guiltless, Guiltless.
Guiltless, Guiltless, Guiltless.
Guiltless, Guiltless.
Guiltless!

Response-ability!

I love this one because it's so empowering when we get it. So far, we've identified the primary driver for all personal experience as **our responses** to people, places, and events. Since all responses from within *are* from within, only we have the control to monitor and adjust what pours forth from inside. Response-ability means exactly what it implies—that in any given moment you have the ability to first feel your response, and then know whether it is from your loving Self or your fearful angry ego. So if there's any question, you'd better take an immediate internal inventory because, unless you are willing to identify your anger as your own ego, **you will remain powerless against it.** Conversely, when you *do* call upon your ability to first identify and then transform all unwanted painful responses, forgiveness and understanding take over, and the guilty hangover evaporates into thin air like magic.

Just the other day, the winter tenant living in the house next door (where our old friends have a summer home) invaded our yard and chewed me out for borrowing something out

of "her" basement. I was flabbergasted, since the day before, she had no problem with me in her basement fixing her dryer as a friendly gesture. I was befuddled with her unfriendly tone as she told me in no uncertain terms that I had "violated her boundaries." Violated her boundaries? For god's sake, Ed (the owner and my friend) and I are in each other's garden sheds and basements every other day getting one thing or another. But with this one, *I was the violator!*

Well, I was pissed. I'll fix her, I thought. "The next time she needs a hand, I'll have plenty to say," I mused.

I'm sure you know the rest. The next day, I wrote what you're reading right now, and it became crystal clear to me that whatever I was upset about had only to do with *my* responses to her. I'm not saying that she wasn't a bit rough, but that had nothing to do with my upset and judgment of her. That was all *my* stuff, and, until I owned up to it, I couldn't really interact with her again with any kind of moral authority, which is the only kind of authority worth having.

So, what could I do? I would no doubt bump into her in a day or so . . . what will I say and how will I say it? Then I remembered: We all have a responsibility to employ our "response-ability."

I don't know but, when the time comes,
I intend to ask.

Then, whatever I say will be appropriate to her
and to me.

I agree not to second-guess.

I agree not to plan.

I agree to allow Love to guide me into learning
instead of another dead end.

Now I have used my ability to adjust my response; my response-ability has "removed the log from my eye." It's soothing to remember here that all learning is meant to be comforting and easy. If it comes hard, there's the old ego again.

Beware of the "Safe" Road
(It's the Most Dangerous Place You Can Be)

Danger, danger . . . that's how we think. We're always looking over our shoulders, keeping vigil on our safety, whether it's in crossing the street or in a business transaction. This is especially true in relationships. We think of people as dangerous, that they will hurt us or take from us, and, of course, nothing has more built-in obstacles than romance. Our egos are expecting things to go wrong on a regular basis, so "on guard" is the order of the day.

But does the watchful ego really keep us safe? I'm afraid not.

In fact, you're always in peril
when protecting yourself from anything.

Protection assumes risk is at hand. Defense expects to engage with attack. Caution in relationships *always* impedes the learning between two people who would otherwise have a chance at intimacy. The mind is so powerful that it can perfectly materialize a frame of mind designed to deflect any incoming unwanted attack, and does so, continuously. Because we *are* always expecting fearful outcomes, we are always engaging in defensive warfare. The troops are ready, the guns loaded, and

General Ego is at the helm ready for action. Now tell me how any humane or loving exchange could survive in that environment?

The problem here is that your fearful expectations are creative and limitless, since they employ your creative and limitless mind. Often, they will actually bring about exactly what you fear! Relationships will backfire and fail, and many other encounters with life in this world may be stunted and limited since they are not born in creativity, but in fear.

Isn't this incredible? How perplexing it is to realize that it is your "safe passage" that puts you in jeopardy, and causes your life to wilt on the vine.

Protection births destruction.
The safe road is hell.

The way out is pure and simple: Do *not* defend yourself. Ask for guidance; ask to be carried. Ask that all outcomes be equitable for all involved. Ask for the willingness to allow Love . . . your true Self . . . to lead the way. Do this, and it is done. Don't ask me how it works, but know that it does. I can't begin to account for the power we have within that knows "what to do, where to go, what to say and to whom" (*ACIM* content). I only know that when we have the courage to ask, it is given us to prosper, love, and heal.

So, as a rule of thumb in life from beginning to end, avoid that "safe" road and "take a walk on the mild side," the "Faith" road . . . See you there!

Heaven and Hell Are
on the Same Street

This is the damnedest thing, but not so hard to understand when we look at everyday experiences. Pick a street, any street, and see how going in one direction will take you to a lovely place, and going in the other might take you to the city dump. It sounds simplistic, but most things in life are that simple. We're the ones that make them complicated.

When directed in a positive way, energy gets you to the right destination, gets things done, solves problems, and heals the wounded. But when we go the other way, we undo good works, hurt people and ourselves, and wreck our lives. By the same principle, an axe can be used to chop wood for the fire, or cut off your own head to spite your face. This gets back to the power of your intention utilizing your mind-power (energy) in order to serve your best interests.

I am frequently asked, though, just how we know what is in our best interest, when to say, "Yes" or "No," when to give or take. Do we engage or keep the distance? Do we try for something or not? These are all worthy questions, but trust the simple process of placing one foot in front of the other, and watch the answers materialize right in front of you.

A few days ago, I took my wife's car to have some scratches removed. The shop owner wasn't there, so his son took over and with his assurances that he knew what he was doing, I left the car for the day. Needless to say, I picked it up that night and it was a disaster. Everything that he could have done wrong, he did. I politely let him know that there was a problem, paid him nothing, and said I'd talk to his dad later in the week.

You guessed it . . . for a few days, I thought maybe I should rehearse what to say, since the last thing I wanted to do was pay for shoddy work. But this time, I remembered . . . don't plan . . . don't script . . . go the positive route . . . go to "heaven," not hell. The next day, I nervously showed up, and what do you think—Dad wasn't there so I was faced with the kid again. He promptly apologized and said that he had explained the whole thing to his father, who agreed to do it all over again—only this time the right way.

I was amazed. The entire debacle was straightened out without my having to say one word. Inside of me, something very powerful had happened. This time, *I* wanted an innocent experience; *I* wanted a solution without anyone having to be guilty of anything. So *I* chose for guidance and wisdom, and the problem was solved. That's exactly what we are being asked to do all the time:

Choose for a change of mind internally, and let the details take care of themselves.

The solution (heaven/innocence) and the problem (hell/guilt) can be brought about in a heartbeat. Be sure you know what you want, then choose for it, and the job is done. Of course, you must trust that your inner guide will never fail you, for if you don't, you have undercut the positive outcomes before they have a chance to manifest. It's always a good idea to check in with your belief system at times like these just to be sure you've taken the right turn on *your* street!

It's All YOU!
(You're Going to Love This Idea)

Go to a place where you live and find a lamp with a removable shade. Take the shade off. Now, take a piece of paper and poke holes in it with an ice pick or sharp pencil.

1. Hold the paper in front of the bulb.

2. Turn on the bulb and see the many points of light shining through.

3. Choose one of those light beams to represent you . . . the others, everyone else.

See . . . there you are, one of billions of rays of light, one of billions in the world.

NOW, remove the paper . . . there is still only *one* blazing light in front of you.

That's who you really are; you are the "One."

You are the one light; you are *not* an individual ray through a pinhole — (that is, however, how you make yourself small, how we all make ourselves small). But when you remember that you are total consciousness, that you are the universe, that you are the singular love-experience always created perfectly in this moment, the *miracle* happens. You'll understand that the light *is* you, and it *is* complete, healed and whole, perfectly innocent and pure. We all have the responsibility to see ourselves this way sooner or later.

In time, this will happen because it must. It must, because the Truth of You cannot be confined.

Love extends by nature.

The Art of Centeredness

Centeredness is not found within your thought system. You can't "think' your way into it. I know that seems like an oxymoron since everything we learn, read, understand seems to occur within the thinking arena, but some things in life, the real essence of life, are not reachable through the mind.

Centeredness is within the realm of the experiential.
It is allowed, not caused.

Look at a recent moment when you felt really good, really on top of things, not frightened, or just plain happy, perhaps from a loving phone call or a bouquet of flowers. In that moment — like magic — you felt wonderful.

How did you do that? Was it the flowers
that made you happy . . . the phone call? Is
there some secret recipe the mind holds for
happiness? Did you "plan" to be happy in
that moment, or "centered" in that moment?

Of course not. It just happened. It happened because *you* let it happen. Your mind was completely out of the picture for that moment, and Love was allowed to be felt without your usual fear, guilt, or distrust. You may think that your mind conjured up "happy" because of the flowers or the phone call, but that's not it. Your mind didn't do a thing, and that's the secret. The more you disengage from using your mind to think your way to peace, the easier it will be to find peace. Peace or centeredness is allowed, not brought about through effort. Remember . . . healing is effortless. Centeredness happens by itself. The less you do, the better.

One day in my office, I asked someone, "What is centeredness?"

"Hmm, well, peace, I guess."

"What's peace?" I asked.

"Love?" she timidly offered.

"Yes, that's it," I said.

"But . . . what's Love?" I asked.

After a long pause she softly admitted, "I don't know."

That's right—she didn't know and neither do we. Love is not explicable. Love is felt; love has ultimate power. Love *is*, but *is not* understood by your mind. So, don't bother trying to muscle it in . . . *it* comes by itself, when *you* let it.

Centeredness will embrace you
whenever you simply allow.

Try it now for a few seconds. Breathe, close your eyes, and . . . *allow.* Feel happy and centered — not from the phone call or the flowers, but because it's the most natural experience you can have. Your love wants to love you; let it. Now, you *are* centered.

"Script *This*!"

What does one usually say when offered a ridiculous deal, or subjected to a snide remark? You think, "F... this, I can do better somewhere else or, *with* someone else." If that's what occurred to you, you're normal. There's no reason to tolerate a no-win relationship with anyone or anything, and, granted, sometimes it's just best to leave the unworkable behind.

But having said that, we are still in charge of all *inner* experiences through our responses, so we must accept authorship of the script we seem to be living. Just like in a play, our lives will "play out" the script for the day.

Last night I had a most painful dream. I was sitting on a high bluff just after a huge winter storm. Snow was heaped up everywhere, right up to the edge of the cliff. Suddenly, an old friend appeared off to the left, got out of his car, hopped on his beautiful white and black speckled horse, and rode over to say hello to me. He perched himself on a huge pile of snow on the bluff right in front of me (he didn't see that he was on the cliff edge). He waved and said, "Hi, John!" Then, horrifically, he and his horse silently slid off the cliff and fell to their death a thousand feet below. I woke up traumatized!

"Oh my God," I thought, "what have I done in this painful dream?" I know enough by now to know that all characters in a dream come from the dreamer, so *I* was the one on the beautiful horse that fell to his death. It was *me* the dreamer that suffered the ultimate loss of love and life in a heartbeat; one second, on a horse in the dazzling snow . . . the next—falling to my death taking the innocent horse with me.

"What the hell's wrong with me?" I thought. "I'm supposed to be the awakened one. How could *I* possibly be having these twisted fantasies coming from my insides, and, more importantly, what am I supposed to do about it?"

Change the script!

And of course, that's true. But for a moment I believed there was something deep within that was out of whack. So I felt "out of whack." It crept up on me in seconds just the way the ego always does. But *this* time, I remembered what was needed—a change—a change so profound that no aftereffects of the dream or its interpretations would remain. I changed my script to read as follows:

The dream left me feeling sick inside, so it must have been false. What is false cannot threaten what is true (my lovability). Therefore, my Love remains intact, unaffected by morbid fantasy, and *I am free*.

I changed the script and wrote in a new direction
that brought with it the guarantee of
    peace and centeredness. The change of feeling was
instant, since all feelings reflect beliefs and thoughts as
they occur. Change your thoughts, unhook from the old
sinking belief system, and provide a baseline of happy
endings. Nothing more is expected or required of you.
Correction is easy and available from your mind, upon
demand.

With this point of view, the meaning of life's outcomes, experiences, and relationships are asking to be
reinterpreted *by* you, *for* you, to loving and holy purpose . . . the loving and holy purpose of your own peace
of mind.

Take the mind-power offered, and be free.

Let's Wrap It Up

Your ego's nuts. And you're nuts whenever you believe what it's saying. Just because your beautiful mind has the potential to think anything, no matter how outlandish, that doesn't mean you have to subscribe to it. Your mind, your "thinking device," is free to think anything it wants, but *you* are bound to principles that separate Truth from illusion.

Life is an eternal conveyer belt. You are standing at the end. Toward you, at light speed, is coming everything that your mind (and everyone else's mind) has thought of and *can* think of. Your job is to sort out the junk (guilt) from the truth (Love) as it arrives at the end of the conveyer right in your lap.

Life is no more complicated than that; remove everything that's not useful and what remains is only Love. And as we have said early on, you can always tell what's true by how you feel just after you "think" it. A good feeling says the thought is true; a bad one says it's not.

Now, it's time to take your assignment very seriously. It's time to stand at the conveyer belt and throw off the junky, guilty, meaningless, self-effacing, demeaning, judgmental, punishing, noncreative bullshit once and for all. Everything remaining is here to help you celebrate your innocence, your love, your nobility and honesty, your courage, your holiness, your whole life — as it was, is now, and ever shall be . . . INNOCENT!

Thank you all for allowing me to share my
happiness with you. God bless you in your
journey toward peace . . .
I'll see you when you get here . . .

Notes

Notes

Notes

Notes

Notes

Notes

Notes

Notes

Notes

Notes